WOODEN SKIS

The Life and Stories of Chic Morton and Early Skiing at Alta.

KIM MORTON

ISBN: 1478155817
ISBN 13: 9781478155812

TABLE OF CONTENTS

DEDICATIONS

I dedicate this little book to all the lovers of Alta, also to my family who encouraged me and helped make this book a reality and who also feel passionate about Alta, to all of you who shared your stories with me. To my husband, Skip Zeller, who always had faith in my ability to write down Chic's stories and spent many hours reading and listening to my stories. I also want to include my technical help; my writing coach; Katey Coeffey and her ideas and suggestions; and to Mary Nowotny, who did the technical editing and thanks for her patience and gentleness.

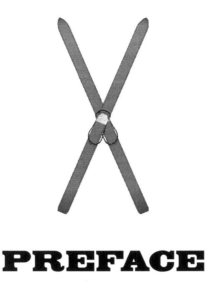

PREFACE

There was a bit of magic, for me, growing up in Alta, Utah, in the, 50's, 60's and '70s. I wanted to capture some of that magic in this book and also tell the story of Chic Morton and many of the people who loved, lived and played at Alto the same time as Chic Alta is a passion for many people, and that includes the Morton family. Being the only child of Chic Morton, who lived and worked at Alta for more than 50 years, I was immersed in that world and wanted to share a bit of this enchantment.

I grew up a child of the snow and mountains and still find winter my favorite season. I ski every day from the moment the snow accumulates enough until it melts away in the spring. Skiing is a way of life to me, not only a sport or job. Today I live with my husband, Skip, in southwest Colorado in the mountains. I had always intended to go back to Alta and live some-day, maybe I will. Our home here in Colorado is beautiful and wild, and I feel very fortunate to have lived in such beautiful and magical places.

After my father, Chic, died in 1997, I began my search for ways to memorialize him in Alta's consolidated memory. As his successor, Onno and Connie, his niece, will remember, I came to them with many different ideas on how to accomplish this task. I wanted the new Collins Chair Lift named "Chic's Chair". I thought it was catchy and fun. The board of directors reminded me that Alta's chairs lifts always have had names that had something to do with mining and that Chic was not a fan of high-speed chairs and the fact that the Collins Chair was such a chair seemed wrong to them. I thought of naming the transfer tow after him. He was always so proud of it. I would've loved to have a ski run named for him, like High Rustler is Alf's High Rustler. Onno was patient with me and said he thought that when they expanded into Grizzly Gully, it would be a good time to name something there after him. I needed to do something now and slowly the idea of a book about his life emerged.

This book has been a project of toil, love and cherished memories. My objective was for my readers to know or remember Chic and what it was like to live in Alta in those early years, to work and raise a family. It is a work of non-fiction, but much of it has come from my own personal memories and thus others may remember them differently.

I was fortunate to have plenty of time when Dad was laid up after his hip operation to ask him questions and get him to tell his story. Some of it I had heard before and yet I learned things that were new. It was one of those quality times I will remember the rest of my life. He asked me what I had in mind with all this information I was getting from him and I told him I was going to write a book. He rewarded me with one of his famous smiles.

I would've loved to include everyone whom knew Chic in this book because I know your stories are important too. Rest assured that I do look forward to hearing those stories at some point in the near future.

Part of this book has to be about the history of Alta. I noticed as I researched and read about the history that not all of it jived. As friends of mine who are historians say, there are the facts and then the way people remember the facts. I included Alta's history as it related to Chic and his life. I hope those of you who are interested in more will use many other wonderful resources to learn more of the richness of Alta's past.

My hope is that all of you reading this will experience the joy and magic of living in Alta and the fun, mischievous and strong character who was Chic.

CHAPTER 1

THE BEGINNING

Take a moment to imagine the sky a brilliant blue and so rich it looked like it had been polished; the snow was deep enough to hide all but a few lumpy forms of cars parked on the only road into Alta. A winter storm had left more than three feet of dry powder snow so light that even with the tiniest wisp of wind these flakes were blown into a swirling dance. A lone man trudged through the snow leaving a hip-deep trough in his wake. Chic Morton was on his way to begin the morning operations of the ski lifts at Alta. The year was 1946. There were few other people about this early morning so the snow was yet untracked. The early sun caught the snow crystals and tiny rainbows played on the surface of the snow. The crystals in the shade of the trees still glistened but with different shades of blue.

Chic carried a shovel to clean off the ramp at the base of Collins Lift, where he and his buddies would coax the lift motor to life, brush the snow off the chairs and load expectant skiers up the mountain. Across the valley and opposite the lifts, the Alta Lodge nestled in the snow and was full of excited skiers ready to experience exquisite turns in the powder. As Chic walked, his breath crystallized in the cold air and he whistled a tune as he began his shoveling.

This was only a small part of the varied life Chic would choose over the next half century at Alta, Utah. His stories and those of other Alta folks tell of the unique life in Alta through the 1940s and into the 1950s when the ski lift towers were made of wood timbers, skis of laminated wood and the men were tough as steel.

Chic Morton was one of the pioneers of early ski area management in the West, specifically Alta, Utah. Chic's history in the ski tourist industry had spanned 39 years when he became the first person honored in the Utah Tourist Hall of Fame on May 23, 1985. Later, he would be awarded the S.J. and J.E. Quinney Award for outstanding achievement and contribution to Utah's Ski Industry. Chic was also instrumental in establishing the first Tramway Board in Utah to standardize the safety and operations of all ski lifts. It is said by more than a few people that Chic Morton's name was synonymous with Alta. It is also said that Alta has a unique personality and it comes from the people who have worked and lived there during their lives. Many of those personalities were directed by Chic. Chic's leadership style was people-oriented and, with his sound management, Alta became known as one of the best managed ski areas in the country during his tenure.

Chic became as much a part of the history of Alta as the miners who first inhabited the canyon in the 1880s. These miners, who dug hundreds of miles of tunnels under the ridges and valleys of Alta, were looking for their fortunes in gold and silver. Before the big mining companies got involved, these early miners used picks and shovels to pry ore from the rocks. Whether by some sort of innate wisdom or luck, they were able to follow tiny veins of silver or gold and extract enough to pack on their mules and lumber down the mountain to the assay office. Then they supported the many saloons, brothels and eateries with their hard earned money. The buildings of 1880s Alta were built from the trees that clung to the steep mountainsides above the town. The un-milled trees were used as timbers in the mine shafts and ties for the rails that moved ore carts from the mines.

Chic's quest for fortune at Alta was more about the beauty and the people than gaining riches. During Chic's time at Alta, most of the digging was for new lift towers that sprouted like inanimate trees bare of boughs which climbed up the mountainsides. These towers turned from wood to steel as the years progressed. The other digging was for foundations of the four ski lodges or the handful of houses that sprung up on the slopes above Alta. The materials for homes were hauled up steep Little Cottonwood Canyon from the Salt Lake Valley.

Chic's history was woven with Alta's like a colorful tapestry. Picture the shades of gold and maroon that adorn the mountain slopes in the autumn and envision Chic taking Alta from the second ski area built in the West with only one chair lift to a world renowned ski area. Now, picture early spring when the snow is just melting and the aspens are budding with tiny green leaves; now allow yourself to see the expansion of the small Alta ski lodge which the Rio Grande Railroad built to compete with the other blossoming ski area of Sun Valley and making it into a warm and inviting place for skiers from all over to come and stay. Visualize, if you will, the abundant colors and varieties of wildflowers that blanket the ground in summer and envision the rich life he created for himself and his family that would last more than five decades. Think about the golden lobbed orbs of aspen leaves in the fall that shimmer with their own light and allow yourself to see how Chic's conservative business philosophy kept Alta a great place where local skiers could afford to ski with their entire family. He and the lift company kept Alta small with not much base area development and with the emphasis on skiing. The entire tapestry that was Chic's life at Alta was his home, his life's work and his love.

Now envision the early days of skiing when it was in its infancy before World War II and its future an open book. The railroads, specifically the Union Pacific, looked at skiing as an excellent way to increase passengers on their trains. The railroads developed special ski trains, called "Rails to Trails," which skiers could board for weekend ski excursions. Skiers could get on a train Friday after work in Los Angeles and arrive in Salt Lake City early enough on Saturday to be on the slopes at Alta. On Sunday evening, exhausted from two days of skiing, they would board the train and be back in LA in time for work, having slept soundly Sunday night dreaming of skiing soft powder snow. Their dreams drifted from blue sky and plenty of sunshine, or turning through deep light snow in the trees while the flakes of a famous Alta snowstorm accumulated quickly around them, knowing that their tracks would be completely covered by the time they came back for the next run.

Early on, the railroads sent a scout to several spots in the West to look for suitable sites. Alta was one of those places. Fred Speyer, who was familiar with Alta and would later become the first general manager of the lift company, guided the representative of the railroad and toured him around Alta. Sun Valley became their ultimate choice but the seed was planted for Alta to grow into a ski area. In 1936, a group of businessmen in Salt Lake City, investigated the idea of acquiring land to develop skiing at the head of Little Cottonwood Canyon. This group was headed by Joe Quinney.

George Watson, a longtime resident of old Alta, had bought up many of the mining claims after the miners had pulled out when the price of ore bottomed. When Joe approached him about his ski area idea, Mr. Watson–or Mayor Watson as he was later called–agreed to sign over his 1,800 acres of land to the Forest Service in exchange for tax relief from those properties. Alf Engen and his brother Sverrre would help lay out the new ski area, as Joe Quinney and his partners organized the Salt Lake Winter Sports Association to begin building lifts for the new ski area which would be located mostly on Forest Service land donated by the "mayor". Later, in 1960 when Fred Speyer hired Chic Morton to take over the lift company, Chic and Joe Quinney would work together to grow Alta into an exceptional skiing experience.

"TIME CHANGES THINGS, EXCEPT THE FEELING."
Alta sales and marketing department marketing slogan

Modern ski areas bustle with activity and noise and not all of it is about the sport of skiing. The mountains still glisten with thousands of snowflakes like white diamonds of winter. The trees still embrace the remnants of the last snow, in their gentle boughs. The quiet of winter is so deep that the tiniest breath of wind, a bird call or a clump of snow falling from a branch is the only sound. The whish of skis moving across the snow, the sense of the combination of gravity, snow and the arc of the skis creates the dance of winter which is timeless.

The passage of time has altered skiing.

Current ski areas bustle with activity and in addition to ski lifts and skiers, there also may be an ice-skating arena, a sledding hill, and possibly a zip line to entertain the tourist who is looking for a winter mountain experience.

Base areas of many of these major ski areas include shopping for clothing and whimsical mountain trinkets, fancy restaurants and coffee shops. Tourists may stay at resorts for five-seven days and ski only two or three days. Besides shopping and dining, they may spend a day snowmobiling, riding a sleigh driven by large-hoofed draft horses or snowshoeing on a wooded trail. Tiny white lights cover every spruce tree and building, giving the area a permanent Christmas feeling. The nighttime experience is as active as daytime as people coming with families from the cities are used to being entertained after the sun sets.

The ski areas today offer many conveniences, like paved parking areas, shuttle buses that keep walking in ski boots to a minimum and chairlifts that transport skiers up the mountain in a state-of-the-art, high speed, chair lift. From here, skiers can choose to ski a groomed trail or a more adventuresome run. If they want to ski untracked powder, crud or moguls, ski areas leave a few un-groomed expert/black runs and maybe several intermediate/blues to test their skills.

Ski equipment has changed dramatically over the years. Modern skis are short and shaped and designed to turn by tipping them on their edges, with very little effort make near perfect arced turns. Skis are fatter than their older cousins and so they float on powder snow like little boats. Modern bindings require skiers only to step in and ski away. They have many safety features that release skiers from the ski if too much torque is applied to their legs.

Ski clothing is waterproof, wind resistant, warm and fashionable. Many skiers choose to wear state-of-the-art helmets instead of ski hats. Ski goggles protect skiers eyes with a myriad of colored lenses for each kind of weather. Skiers prone to being cold can purchase boot heaters to keep their feet warm, hand warmers to slip into their gloves and a wonderful invention called a neck gator that comes up over the skiers face and protects it from cold and snow.

At many resorts, there are high end restaurants on the mountain where they serve gourmet food with white linen table clothes and china plates and skiers can take off ski boots at the door and step into slippers for comfort.

In this new millennium, skiing is not as simple as it once was and skiers expect a lot more of ski areas. They want faster lifts, groomed runs plus amenities on and off the slopes. They ski fast and want to ski as many runs as possible and, when they are finished skiing, they are not satisfied putting their feet up in front of a roaring fire; they want other things to occupy their time.

The sport of skiing competes with popular cruise ships that offer every kind of activity and food one can imagine, along with trips to shore in exotic ports. The other large competitor for the family of skiers is theme parks with thousands of different rides and experiences all in the same venue. It is not surprising that skiing has had to adapt to keep people coming to the sport of skiing.

Skiing isn't as wild, unpredictable and adventuresome as it was in the "good old days". Back then people's expectations were simple; it was all about slipping and sliding in a winter environment with the added benefit of having uphill transportation. In those early days, ski lifts gave skiers transportation up the mountain followed by the thrill of their own unique experience making their way down the runs.

Good skiers are still as graceful and elegant as they swoop down the mountain using the terrain as their own special playground as in the days of old; it is simply a different playground. Of course, skiing was much more of a novelty back then; after all, it was a fairly new sport. It isn't surprising that there is a surge in popularity of backcountry skiing where skiers hike up mountains with climbing skins strapped to their skis and then ski untracked powder for as long as they have the energy to hike uphill. This climb and ski is much like it was before skiers had rope tows and ski lifts.

The early skiers were an adventuresome group. They were looking for the fun and excitement of playing on the mountain, covered either in untracked powder, crud, or lumpy, uneven snow. The spectacular views of the peaks in their winter cloaks were an added benefit. There were wooden trail signs to give skiers a general idea where to ski and much of the fun was being able to navigate down the mountain under their own power. Food was what they brought in their knapsacks, and restrooms were often an outhouse.

In the early days of skiing, it took new skiers several seasons of lessons and practice to ski parallel turns on intermediate/blue slopes. With modern equipment and grooming, skiers of average athletic ability can quickly progress to steeper slopes and varying conditions. When they had only basic grooming equipment, novice skiers often struggled in deep powder or junky snow. Now all beginner/green runs are buffed out with a smooth "corduroy" surface that makes the most timid skier successful.

Skiing in the western states is a very young sport. Before the 1940s sliding on skis was only something a few people used for transportation in the high snowy mountains. These early skis were actually called "snowshoes" because they were used to walk over the snow in shoes attached to skis without sinking. Over time, when ski lifts began to pop up, skiing became more popular. At first, there were only rope tows, which was an improvement from walking or sidestepping up the mountain. By the 1940s, the U.S. ski areas had 19 chairlifts and as many as 300 rope tow only hills.

A ski day started with the adventure of driving up to the ski mountain. There were no SUVs with fancy snow tires and four-wheel drive. The old heavy cars crept up steep and curvy two-lane roads, often snowpacked and slick. Heaters and defrosters on those early cars didn't always keep up with the need, so seeing and staying warm were both challenging.

Once at the mountain, these brave skiers tied the laces of their leather boots as tight as they could and grabbed their long (the ideal ski length was measured by a person's height and the full extension of one arm) heavy, wooden skis off the top of the car, then slog through deep snow to the ticket office. The price of lift tickets was cheap by our modern standards–a couple of dollars for a day of skiing– but back then people didn't make as much money either. The next arduous task was putting the ski boot into the binding. Everything had to be just so for the lever to close and secure the cable that connected the boot to the ski. A little snow stuck on the toe of the boot or under the lever could cause problems. Next there were the safety straps that kept the ski connected to the skier if they tumbled and their ski came off. The entire time the skier was performing this feat while bending over their skis.

At many of the resorts, there were ramps or a hill to climb to the lift, which allowed for the many feet of snow that accumulated during the winter to keep the bottom terminal from being buried. Often, people's first adventures skiing were trying to navigate uphill without sliding backwards or sideways. Once this small mountain was climbed, they were ready to load the chair.

Early on, most lifts were single chairs and pretty slow. Slowness on a sunny day was fun and offered a great way to view the mountains. But on a snowy day with the wind blowing, skiers might unload the chairlift covered with several inches of snow and ice along with frozen fingers and toes. Before they started down, they would brush the snow off their nylon jackets with either wool or leather gloves.

Ski pants of wool may have soaked up a bit of melted snow on the way up and felt a bit soggy. Now skiers were ready to pull their goggles down and take off making huge swooping turns that kept their speed under control on the ungroomed and often bumpy, rough conditions. Warming huts were just that–a place to go to warm your fingers and toes. A wood stove was the heat source, and most people brought their own food.

Though there are significant differences between early skiing and what it is today, there is also timelessness surrounding skiing. The snow and the mountains are as they have always been, perfect. The absolute blue of the winter sky and the sun shimmering on the snow crystals hasn't changed. The absolute thrill of the feeling of skis sliding on the mountain in harmony with the natural world is still the same. There is still the sensation of working with gravity and speed while transporting oneself down a mountain.

A few more buildings have sprung up over the last 50 years since Chic started working at Alta, but what hasn't changed, is the feeling that man is but a visitor and that the mountains and Mother Nature are supreme. A large snowstorm in February still halts human activity until the threat of avalanches can be controlled by explosives. The buildings become insignificant when they are buried under feet of snow. The power of the snow to destroy has also not changed. The modern snow safety and bombing has helped, but the threat of avalanches still hovers over the valley.

My Dad, Chic Morton, was one of those early adventurers. He was willing to immerse himself in this mountain environment and community. He invested more than 50 years of his life to living in Alta and helping create an outstanding ski resort. To say that his work at Alta was all-consuming would be an understatement. The Alta Lodge was six months of constant attention; he was present at his office taking care of the ski area six days a week. On the seventh, he would drive to Salt Lake City to meet with Joe Quinney, president of Alta Ski Lifts, for lunch and to discuss business. He then would do errands for the company and come home. He called this his day off. It actually was a work day with a slightly different focus, though he could sleep in a little longer on those Tuesday mornings.

It took an adventuresome type of person to work at this fledgling ski area, to deal with the many feet of snow, the lift motors and the people. When Chic was in his late 70s, he stated in an interview, "In those days, Alta was about wooden lift towers, wooden skis and men of steel."

CHAPTER #2

CHIC'S EARLY YEARS

I t is my belief that in order to arrive as productive adults we need to benefit from the jour-
ney of our childhood and early years. It is in those years that the sowing of attributes like
kindness, humor and seeking adventure are honed for maturing as the years accumulate.
So a story about Chic needs to include his early years.

One of my only visions of my Dad as a baby comes from a black and white photograph in a
gold oval frame that peers down at me from the top of our stairs. The photo is about 12 inches
high and, behind the protective glass, peers out an infant in a white christening dress. Already
his eyes twinkle and his tiny smile reflects an indication of what he will become as a man. The
infant is as bald as Chic became in his late twenties, though he had a rich head of brown curly
hair in between. Chic had one of those magical faces, that when he smiled, it involved his entire
face. The reverse was true when he frowned. He loved to laugh and, as the years of out door
living creased lines in his handsome face so did the laughter lines deepened. Chic was an opti-
mistic man who believed that dancing, skiing, horses and fishing could cure anything.

Chic also loved to sing. Visualize a restaurant full of people. My wedding party is sitting at
a long table. Though we weren't the only ones there, we took up about one third of the space.
Just before we were served our meals, my father announced that he had something for me and
John, my first husband. Still sitting, he took a deep breath and in his rich voice, he began to

sing. I don't remember the words to the song but I do know that it was a love ballad. As he sang, the dining room became silent and all the occupants stopped and listened. I know there was not a dry eye in the place when he finished. I believe that it was the first time I really saw my father as the amazing man he was and not just my Dad. Without a hint of self-consciousness, he was able to tell a room of family and strangers about what love meant to him in song.

The power of love is also what produces offspring, and each of us begins our lives as the creation of two unique people. We are products of our environment and of the influence of those around us. Chic was no exception. He grew up during the Depression and accordingly he knew how to live a frugal life. He appreciated the simple things and he had a firsthand knowledge of the importance of personal health.

In the summers when I was a child, he and my mother would take a walk after dinner. The summers at Alta were so short that each day was something to be treasured. The stunted growing season meant that, as soon as the snow melted, green things burst forth, grew and flowered quickly. Our nightly walks involved observing the almost daily changes. Chic would often point out a deer nibbling grass at the edge of the meadow or how tall the skunk cabbage had become. He loved to walk and hike, and because of his accident at the age of 12 when he was hit by a truck, he never took walking for granted. Life was a precious thing to him.

His growing-up story sets the foundation of the adventuresome person he would become as an adult. To Chic, life was a smorgasbord of choices. He was willing and excited to jump into almost anything-from bartering his bicycle for a horse to selling cars, learning how to ski and vesting his life at a ski area. I don't think there were many things that Chic said "no" to.

His experiences helped him become a shrewd businessman. He learned from his work what succeeded in business and what didn't. He soon realized that the customer ruled in business. Later, when he took over the management of Alta Ski Lifts, he wasn't as interested in what the other ski areas were doing but what would work for the unique Alta skier, his customer.

Charles Brunner Morton was born November 24, 1916, in Salt Lake City, Utah to William Jason Morton and Grace Brunner Morton. Charles was their firstborn and, Jean, his brother, would follow a few years later. Chic describes his early childhood as being enjoyable. The Mortons didn't have a lot, but the boys were well taken care of and led a pleasant life. They played hard and worked hard. There was food on the table and a warm, dry place to sleep.

Not many people called Chic Charles, except his mother and later his mother-in- law, Dorothy Norpell. Chic suited him much better, with his mischievous smile and flashing blue eyes. Charles was just a bit too formal. His brother Jean wasn't allowed to call him Chic and would get a belt in the arm from Chic when he tried. Jean would tease him and call him Chicky Chase and then have to run off to keep from being slugged. I believe that the name Chic came from his dear friend Emily, who was found of calling him "Chico". It soon was shortened to Chic. Those who knew him in the ski business all knew him as Chic.

The Morton family was very familiar with physical challenges so it wasn't a surprise that Chic didn't allow his later accident and accompanying limp to stop him from doing much of anything. He had grown up watching his parents deal with such issues.

When the boys were growing up, William was a letter carrier for the Post Office. One winter, William fell during his mail route and broke his arm. It didn't heal properly and became a chronic problem for him. Eventually they had to remove the bone in his arm. Later he had a stroke and finally died of a massive cerebral hemorrhage in the fall of 1935, when Chic was a senior in high school. William had originally wanted to be a doctor. He was in medical school when his eyes began to fail and he dropped out. His medical problems were a struggle for the small family but they managed. Grace and the boys weren't afraid of hard work and they brought in extra cash where they could, selling eggs, having a paper route or selling apple cider. While William was in the hospital, Grace would visit him faithfully. She had no car so she took streetcars and buses there and back again.

Grace was born in Elizabeth, Colorado, on a ranch. She was afflicted with what was called "St. Vitas Dance" back then and is now known as Chorea which is associated with rheumatic fever. It is a disease characterized by rapid, uncoordinated jerking movements in the face, feet and hands. Because of this, she wasn't able to help around the ranch and was unable to attend school. The therapy they used for her was a small amount of arsenic daily. Finally her family sent her to live with her Uncle Cully and Aunt Hannah in Salt Lake City. Grace had resigned herself to the fact that she would probably never marry. William was their postman and he saw her almost every day. I imagine them having a few brief conversations in passing and, after a time, he became very taken with her and convinced her to marry him. Grace lived to a ripe old age of 84. She was a dynamic and spunky woman who knew how to take care of herself and her boys. William, on the other hand was a very easy-going individual. It seems that Chic mostly took after his mother.

After William was forced to retire due to his health, the family moved to a house on Conway Court, 2769 S. and 9th East, in Salt Lake City which had a nice yard and orchard. The entire family worked hard in the orchard to bring in extra money; they sold both apples and cider. Grace needed to drink goat's milk for a stomach problem, so the Mortons bought some goats. Who knows whether the boys tormented the goats more or the other way around? They stayed in that house until Chic was almost 9 years old and then they moved to 45th South in Murray.

William's intention, once they moved, was to sell chickens to supplement their income. The expenses were too great and the Mortons got to a point where they could no longer afford to live in that house so they moved to an apartment on 1st West, where Grace lived until she moved into a nursing home near the end of her life.

Grace and William were both hard working people who taught their sons the benefits of persistence and dedication. Both boys were aware that physical infirmities presented limitations but they were taught to treat them as challenges instead of obstacles.

CHAPTER 3

WORK AND EDUCATION

Managing a ski lift company with 100+ employees who live on-site and need to be feed three meals a day is challenge enough. Now add five departments–lifts, snow machines and shop, ski patrol and snow safety, ski school, and administration, all of whose needs differ and require many skills and experiences to do a good job. Add to that the operation of a ski lodge, which has its own unique challenges, and you have quite a complex job.

The lodge added a bit more spice to his jobs, along with managing workers he had to feed guests and employees three meals a day, make sure the furnace and plumbing were working, know the comings and going of the guests all the while keeping costs down and revenues up. On top of that his job entailed interacting with people from all over the world with many needs and expectations. From early life forward, Chic's wide variety of jobs and work experiences were the training ground for his future work at Alta.

Chic's first job was as a paper boy. He worked for the *Salt Lake Telegram*, a non-Mormon paper. Like most boys, he rode his paper route on his bicycle about seven miles. One Sunday morning as he was nearing the end of his route, his mind was wandering toward what he would do when he got home, maybe some fishing. As he threw his last paper he noticed a boy his age riding his horse in the pasture near his home. Chic pulled his bike over and started quizzing the boy about his horse. He leaned his bike on the fence and climbed into the pasture. The boy let him ride double with him as they trotted and galloped across the field. Chic was hooked. The other boy was intrigued with Chic's bike and so—after extensive negotiations, for which Chic later became famous for, an even trade was made—a bike for a horse. If his mother, Grace, and his father, William, were surprised at their son's trade they didn't show it and only reminded him that a horse was a bit more of a responsibility than a bike. This horse's name was Belle.

He rode that horse on his route winter and summer for as long as he had a paper route and then traded the horse back for his bike, on which he would later have his accident and dislocate his hip. Another story Chic told about Belle was that he would ride him to see a friend on State Street and then tie the reins over his neck and tell him to go home and off he would go. When he would wander into the yard, Grace would open the gate and he would go to the pasture to wait until Chic was ready for another ride.

Chic's mode of transportation changed when his uncle helped him find a Model T Ford at age 16. Later he bought another one with a touring body, and though it had been rolled it had a good engine. So, between the two cars he had a pretty decent one. This was probably the start of his short career as a used car salesman.

He and Joe Coby started a used car business in which they would buy a car, fix it up and sell it. During the war, they bought old big cars that were no longer popular because of gas rationing and then sold them to military personnel who weren't affected by rationing.

Chic started high school at East High School in Salt Lake City. He didn't like it, so he moved to West High School and was able to get student tickets to ride the trolley car. Things worked out much better for him there and graduated in the middle of his senior year, and his uncle got him a scholarship to Latter-day Saints School of Business. He studied accounting and business management, which would come in handy as he managed the Alta Lodge and Alta Ski Lifts Company.

Before he left high school, the counselor told him there was a need for stenographers, so Chic took courses in spelling and letter writing. It was during the Depression, and Chic was unable to get a job, he was determined, and so he walked up and down the streets asking for work. The Goodyear service store hired him, and he soon was a bookkeeper and cashier in the budget department; later he went to the district office. Goodyear had stores in Ogden and Provo. One day, when Chic and another man were on their way to the Ogden store, they stopped at Hill Air Force Base. On a whim, Chic applied for a job and was hired in the teletype department. He was involved in training other teletype operators but, as the men were drafted one by one, they were replaced by women. Chic commented that they were great workers but would fight between themselves. He finally quit the base because of the "bureaucratic bullshit" and also because Goodyear wanted him back. He worked for six months for them and then quit to sell used cars with Joe Coby.

Chic had many jobs over the years and he worked hard. He knew what it was like to have very little and he felt blessed that he had work and could earn money. He learned many skills that he would blend into his future work at Alta. When he started working at Alta, he found his niche. He often said that Alta was the best thing that ever happened to him.

CHAPTER 4

FIRST TRACKS

It takes a skier to manage a ski area and a successful ski lodge. Only a skier knows the true nuances of skiing and what skiers want. Chic didn't have any control over the quantity or quality of snow that blessed the Alta ski slopes, but he knew plenty about customer service and friendly employees who enjoy their work. He realized it was just as important to have a comfortable and warm place on the mountain to rest and regain some of the calories consumed by hours skiing in the cold. The Watson Shelter which was built just above the bottom of the Germania Lift, was named after Mayor Watson, was and still is–though much more modern–one of those places. Later as the "backside" evolved, Collins Grill and the Alpenglow Restaurant appeared. From Chic's humble beginnings, he realized that all the families in the Salt Lake Valley needed the opportunity to ski at a price they could afford, and this was a reality at Alta when Chic was at the helm. Later, when Chic's successor, Onno took over he established a program called "ski free after three" for local families, which has been a huge success and has guaranteed that families could still ski even during economic downturns.

Chic may have learned how to ski by trial and error, but he knew what skiers wanted and needed because he himself was a skier. With his other business experience, he knew that numbers were important but the best moneymaker was a happy and satisfied skier. People came to

Alta to ski, to meet interesting people and to have fun. Chic's management of the Alta Lodge created just the atmosphere to encourage this, and his lift policies were based on taking care of skiers.

Chic's life before Alta and skiing revolved around horses. It was—and would be—one of his great life passions. On many weekends, he and his friends Adrien and Emilie Segil would explore with horses up into the canyons above the Salt Lake Valley.

Picture a warm summer day and, before the dew on the grass in the horse pasture had evaporated, Chic and his favorite friends would saddle their horses and ride up into the steep canyons on the east side of Salt Lake City. Tucked into their saddle bags would be lunch, treats for the horses, a flask of booze and rain slickers. The miles would melt away as they rode up into the high alpine country. The noise of the steep and rocky creeks cascading toward the valley kept them company. The vegetation changed as they climbed—the trees were fewer while the flowers became more numerous and colorful. Finally, they would emerge where the glaciers had cut large bowls with peaks surrounding them like majestic guards. There, next to a more passive creek, they would dismount and enjoy not only gourmet sandwiches but alpine views that stirred their souls.

Chic, Emilie and Adrien, a ski day at Alta.

Those summer days would melt away like spring snow, and they would ride home satiated and pleasantly tired.

Even as the snow piled high in the mountains, they still rode as far as they could up those glaciated canyons. The golden lobed orbs of aspen leaves would have mostly fallen to the ground and snow had started to accumulate up on the peaks when they began to notice cars driving by with skis. This intrigued them. Maybe, when the snow was too deep to ride, they could ski? The thought brewed in their minds until, one sunny day in December, they borrowed some equipment and off they went up Big Cottonwood Canyon. These three young, energetic and athletic people in their 30s looked forward to a different adventure–after all, how hard could it be?

They parked their car and watched as a few skiers swooped down, making graceful turns. They noticed that several others had their skis in a triangle shape as they plowed their way down, often with frightened expressions on their faces. Ready to go, the three friends struggled tightening the laces of their boots. It was Chic's bright idea to climb up the hill higher than any of the other skiers. So, carrying their skis, they enjoyed the bright sunlight which reflected off the snow and the dazzling blue sky. Though they were familiar with the way the bindings worked, it took some time to get everything ready. Chic was sure he didn't need to use that awkward snowplow and would keep his skis parallel. I imagine that Chic was the first one to shove off down what had looked like a small hill with his skis pointing straight down into the valley.

At this point, I need to mention that, when Chic was 12 years old, he dislocated his hip after a truck hit him while he was riding his bicycle. The result was a several-inch difference in his leg lengths and a pronounced limp. He had compensated over the years, but his balance would always be challenged; however he didn't let his "bum" leg stop him or slow him down. When Chic pointed those long wooden boards down that hill, which seemed to have grown into a precipice, he was probably a bit off balance. He fell several times, laughing and struggling back up after learning that the skis did indeed need to be across the hill in order to stand up. His speed kept increasing and, when he was nearing the parked cars and out of necessity, he pushed his skis sideways to keep from landing on the car and surprised himself that he actually stopped. He was thrilled and laughed heartily and encouraged his friends with, "Hey, it's easy, come on down."

His two friends had similar experiences and, learning from their mistakes, soon were able to navigate the small hill. After several hours, they were making turns by shoving their skis from side to side, which enabled them to keep their speed down and actually stop when they wanted. The three of them were hooked and so started a 50-plus -year love affair with skiing and the lifestyle that accompanied it. Chic skied until his hip replacement at age of 70; Emilie skied until she was 80; and Adrien skied until he was hit by a car riding his bike in his 80s and died of his injuries.

Chic tried skiing again after his hip replacement when he was 70 and found that when the surgeon had lengthened his femur to make it the same as the other leg, he no longer could stay in balance. He had skied for years with different length legs and now things didn't work as well for him. He kept falling. It was discouraging. He even went out with Alf Engen, his lifetime friend and head of the Alta Ski School, to see if he could magically make things work. Alf, who has spent his life teaching and encouraging all ages and abilities of skiers, felt he had let his old friend down when he wasn't able to adapt Chic's new body to skiing.

 After that, I took him out and, with some laughs and curses we decided skiing would no longer work for him. The technique he had perfected with his shorter leg wasn't working anymore, and when I tried to take him back and teach him the basics so that his new hip and balance point could adjust, he wasn't able to make the transition. Chic's entire body had adapted to the shorter leg–his pelvic bone was tilted and all the muscles around it had shortened. The new hip gave Chic relief from pain but played havoc with his balance.

This first ski experience with Adrien and Emilie on those early slopes was the beginning of his lifelong passion for skiing and Alta. He would encounter many obstacles during his time at Alta, but his stubborn resolve and creative intellect would always find a path around those daunting hindrances–whether they were personal or professional; he rarely gave up.

Chic had always been willing to try anything, once. While away at school in Colorado, I had taken up cross-country skiing. During a trip back to Alta, I raved so much about my experiences that Chic decided to try it. He bought some skis and out we went on a snowy evening after he came home from work. He thought it might be a great way to get some exercise after working at his desk all day.

We started off by gliding down the snow covered summer road toward Albion Lift. All went well, so up the Crooked Mile ski run we climbed until we got back to the summer road and were about a half mile above the house. The snow was perfect for climbing–just cold enough that our skis clung to the snow and up we went. The mountains were alit with alpenglow as the storm moved out. The peach-colored peaks stopped us for a moment of awe before we started down the road. There were few ski tracks, and the path was very narrow. I wanted him to go first so I could keep an eye on him but, he declined and followed me instead. The snow was perfect for the descent, with just enough fresh snowfall to keep our speed down. With a push of my poles, I glided off. I was able to keep my skis in the track as the speed increased enough to be thrilling but not scary. I was having the time of my life. Remembering Dad, I looked behind me once and there he was, looking a little uncomfortable but still gliding along. The cross-country skis at that time were very skinny and long and, taking into consideration that the heel of the skier was not attached, it was always a challenge with balance not to mention Dad's uneven legs. As the alpenglow faded from the peaks, I turned and looked back up the road again. Dad was gone. No trace. I quickly turned my skis into the powder and stopped, stepped around and hurried back up the road. There he was, planted headfirst in the deep snow, with both of his skis under his body. By the time I got there to help, he had evacuated his head and was spitting out snow. I started to laugh and was able to ask him between giggles if he was okay. "Damn ski got stuck in the soft snow and pulled me in too," he said with a smile and snow all over his face. The rest of the trip down the road was uneventful until we stopped above the house. There was a steep incline to get us back home, but I was convinced that the snow was deep enough that we could point our skis straight down and our speed wouldn't increase too much, as I hadn't gotten to the part of the lesson about turning yet. That proved correct for me because I weighed less, but Chic's speed increased and he kept going past the house, the entire time yelling, "How do I stop?" as he zipped by the kitchen window where his wife, Jean, inside making dinner, watched his flying descent. I helped dig him out after his tumble that indeed did stop him.

After dusting off the snow, we walked into the house and, when Jean inquired how it went, he said, "That is enough of that," though he was smiling. It was a fun adventure but, between his balance issues and not having time to learn a new form of skiing, he was done. He gave those skis to his old friend Dottie Weaver, who just recently gave them back to me so they have come full circle.

Long before his experience with Adrien and Emilie at Alta, Chic had experimented with skiing. Chic's brother Jean remembers that, when Chic was in high school he made a pair of skis in shop. In the pasture behind their house, he made a jump and got his first small taste of sliding and getting air. What I would give to have that pair of skis today. I imagine his taking time to shovel the jump and pack the hill. I wonder about when he became airborne on his first jump–was he scared or exhilarated or both before he landed?

Chic's "first tracks" on skis and into the culture of Alta was just a single small step toward a remarkable history where he left more than ski tracks–he left his legacy. Two of his nieces, Connie Marshall and Annette Carhart, still work at Alta. Connie is Alta's public relations person and keeps the flavor of Alta alive to the skiing public. She skis with reporters and dignitaries she keeps Alta's advertising fresh and enticing; and she travels to many ski shows to represent Alta. Connie first came to Alta from Newark, Ohio when she was 12 years old to spend time with the Mortons. That summer she got to know her Uncle Chic. She commented that Chic was very busy with his summer work but she quickly fell in love with his fun-loving spirit and twinkle in his eyes. She came back after her high school graduation and met Chic's second wife, Jean, for the first time. After college, she again made a trip out west to see me in Gunnison. She thought she would stay and work, but the small town didn't offer what she needed and, when Jean and Chic came one weekend to see me they encouraged her to come back to Alta and get a job for the winter. She applied with the ticket office and, in two years, was the department head, working directly for her Uncle Chic. As she stated to me, her relationship with him shifted a lot since she had to report directly to him and, though they had a professional relationship, she and her family still spent time with Chic and Jean on holidays at the Alta house. Connie's first winter at Alta was in 1974 and she still works there 38 years later. She married George Marshall, who worked on the lifts, and had their first child, Maxine, still living at Alta. After their twins, Audrey and Bradly, were born, they moved to Salt Lake City and larger accommodations for the growing family. She and George's hearts are still in Alta.

Annette is the administrative and sales supervisor in the ski school. She is the behind-the-scenes person who makes the ski school function—whether it is lessons and ticket sales, payroll or private lesson assignments. She also helps create the ski school brochure. Annette started working with Jean, my step-mother, in the ski school at the sales desk in 1981 part-time. In 1988, when Jean retired, Annette took over. Another ski industry member is Annette's son Will, who works for Doppelmayr/Garavent lift company and is one of the electricians for the newly built lifts. He also is on site for the installation. He follows in the footsteps of his father, Michael Carhart, who worked in the lift building industry for years.

Though my involvement at Alta is one of recreation as Chic's daughter, I have carried on the skiing way of life for another 50 years. Besides sharing my passion for skiing with others through teaching, I have worked as a ski instructor and trainer both at my home area, Purgatory, and traveled in Colorado, New Mexico and Arizona, training their resorts' instructors. In 1989, I was honored with Colorado Ski Instructor of the Year. Chic was pretty proud and made sure that the Salt Lake City papers carried an article about that award. I became one of three female ski school directors in the country at that time and also started one of the first all, 'women', only ski school lessons that still operates today. I was able to take that concept to the Professional Snowsports Instructors of America and now most ski areas have women-only ski programs.

Chic's legacy in the ski business is continuing through his family and those people he worked with and in all the associated memories.

CHAPTER #5

SKIING AND HORSES

What was the connection between horses and snow for Chic? He was passionate about both and, wanted to make sure they were both in his life, always.
Chic didn't stop riding horses after he discovered skiing. In fact, he bought a
stable. He and a partner took care of a few horses for other people and they had many of their
own. Spending time with horses was about as good as it gets, he thought. The business also
included a club or bar. Chic loved socializing but, after a day taking care of horses, the last thing
he wanted to do was deal with drunks. So, his partner dealt with that aspect of the business.
Chic felt he had a full life and was content. Interestingly enough, fate usually has a say about
any kind of stasis. A friend of his stopped by the stable and offered him a job working on the
lifts at Alta. His first reaction was, " No", he had to take care of those beasties. But Fred Spier,
knew Chic well enough to realize that he wouldn't turn down something new, suggested that
he pick Dad up each morning at the stable and drop him off each evening so he could feed the
horses. The idea of being up at Alta working swayed him and he said, "yes." It made for long
days all winter, but Chic was immersed in two things he loved, so what could be better? The lure
of the mountains and snow was enough so off he went.

Working on those old lifts wasn't always easy. When a storm would howl and blow all night
long the chairs on the lift would be buried. The operators dug out the lift line so the chairs

could move forward again. The lift towers were wooden and not as tall as the modern ones because everything was built by hand and the lumber to build those lifts was manhandled into place only after a death defying trip up the mountain on a rocky step road. This is where these hard-core construction workers earned their nickname "Men of Steel". Sometimes, after the lift line was dug out for the chairs to ascend, wind would deposit all the snow back in the track and off the men would go with shovels and start again. Another example of how tough these men were is that the top operator didn't zoom up the mountain on a snowmobile. He strapped on ski skins and walked up, which is a good way to get warm first thing in the morning but not very fast. The motors on the ski lifts were often old, persnickety and temperamental. Those were the practical and mechanical issues of lift operation, but after these tough guys got the lift running, they dealt with the skiers, loading chairs all day. Skiers, even those above novice, often had challenges getting on and off the lift. The operator was there to help, untangle and prop up the skier before they could load. People skills were a must, and patience didn't hurt either. Hey, but what better office to work in even if the work gets a bit old. Imagine a novice skier who, after sliding backward several times, finally makes it up the ramp and, out of breath, slides toward the chair but, not paying very close attention to the spacing of the chairs, is late arriving and the chair bonks him and sends him flying to the side. Unfortunately for the lift operator, this particular skier had trouble getting up too and he is in the way of the on-coming chairs. The lift has to be stopped so the skier can be helped up and loaded. I wonder how his trip down the mountain was when he had such a challenge getting on the lift?

Back in those days, they would shut down the lifts for lunch, and one such day in mid-winter, the boys went up to start the Peruvian Chair Lift. The base was near the original Watson Shelter at the top of the ridge between Peruvian Gulch and Alta. It took awhile for the top operator to climb up in the new snow, so Chic was left at the bottom shoveling. The blowing snow had lifted enough that, when Chic looked up toward the top, he could just see the lift shack and the operator's ski tracks so he knew he was inside. As he watched, there was a puff of smoke and the top operator jumped out of the lift shack as flames followed him out the door. This was the end of the Peruvian Lift and its wooden towers.

I am not sure how many actual turns Chic was able to etch in that light powder snow that winter but he was hooked on the life at Alta.

CHAPTER #6

WAR INTERVENES

On December 7, 1941, things changed all over the United States. Men were shipped off to war, leaving women to take over many of the jobs that men had held. The people left at home did what they could to support the war effort. Alta kept losing its lift maintenance men to the war, so the lifts shut down temporarily. It was on a day when Fred Speyer was up with his wife, Coke, skinning up and skiing, and the fact that those lifts were shut down bothered him so much he jumped in and took the job so the lifts at Alta were in operation again.

Chic and Adrien were up in Brighton skiing the day Pearl Harbor was bombed. When Chic was asked if anything particular stood out in his mind about that day he said,

"Everybody up there was shocked of course and we immediately, as soon as we got the word, got in our car and headed down to the valley. The next morning I got a phone call from Hill Field; they wanted me up there that night. I went up and was there to prepare for the war."

Chic was unable to participate in combat due to the injury he sustained when he had been hit by a truck at age 12. He wanted to do his bit to help the war effort in whatever way he was able so he became a supervisor of the Teletype Department at Hill Air Force Base at the start of the war and then was moved to senior supervisor of Property Accounting on the IBM machines.

The accident dislocated his hip and by the time they relocated it, he had lost much of the blood supply. When he came out of the hospital, he was fitted with a steel brace and told he would never walk without it. Chic was a stubborn and determined man and he went through some terrible times thinking he wouldn't be able to walk normally again. With a little encouragement from a family doctor who told him to walk out as far as he could from the house every day and then walk back, it wasn't long before he threw the brace away. Even so he was left with a marked limp. By the time he had his hip replaced at age 70 his leg was six inches shorter than the other one. It never stopped him from skiing, hiking, horseback riding, mountain climbing and fishing. He often said the only thing he couldn't figure out how to do was water ski with his bum leg, and technical rock climbing was also too much of a challenge.

Chic had struggled as a young man with self-esteem while his leg was in a brace after his accident. When he was finally able to walk without his brace, he often got depressed about the limited use of his leg. I'm sure this is what made him so determined to do so many other things during his life. He also never would abide with excuses by others why they couldn't do something. An example of this strength at overcoming obstacles is obvious in the following story. He was in high school and it was spring and the class dance was coming up. He wanted to go with a date and dance. He even knew the girl he wanted to go with and was scared to death to call her. He sat at the phone table, finger poised over the dial sweating with clammy hands. Finally he got up his courage to call, and she accepted. She didn't seem to mind his limp, and he was a great dancer. He was a charmer, and they had a wonderful evening. From this point forward Chic continued his love of dancing for the rest of his life.

Emilie Segil and he would go to the Sky Room at the Hotel Utah and dance away the evening. It was during the Depression, they would bring their own booze the cover charge was $1. They would have a delightful evening, twirling around the dance floor. One of the other places they loved to dance was at Salt Air, a dance floor on the edge of the Great Salt Lake, where the big bands were featured on Monday nights.

While working at Hill Air Force Base, Chic skied every chance he got and went up to Alta Lodge where he stayed, in the dorms, and skied the next day. However, the first few months after the U.S. declared war, he was on duty seven days a week and wasn't able to ski, which worked out fine as long as Alta was closed.

Alta's skiing was not only used as a recreation destination but, in the fall of 1941, a group of paratroopers were brought to Alta for training. With the help of Dick Durrance, who was the ski school director at that time, and a talented bunch of instructors, the soldiers were divided into ten groups. Some of them became very competent skiers some were in survival mode; and others didn't get skiing at all. Several of the soldiers were sent home with broken legs due to their skiing adventures. This winter warfare group was never put to use, though the men involved never forgot the time they spent serving their country at Alta, learning to ski.

While Chic served his country at home, his younger brother Jean served in the war in the Army Air Corps as a tech sergeant stationed in England. He gave technical administrative support in the Army Air Corps, a branch of the Army. He met and married his wife, Thelma, who traveled to the U.S. by ship and then took the train to meet him in Salt Lake City. They were married in King's Lynn, England.

When the war ended, people were ready to ski and came back. Chic was again skiing and working on the lifts.

Chic and Maxine after ski skinning up the mountain.

CHAPTER #7

LOVE

Chic loved his life. He thought he had it all. He loved his work, and living among the snowy mountains was a plus. He still got to ride and be around horses, and he had met some interesting and fun people working at Alta.

As fate would have it, a young woman from Newark, Ohio, was going to challenge his bachelor ways. Early in the winter of 1949, Maxine Norpell and her friend, Anne, arrived at Alta to experience skiing life and work at the Alta Lodge. Maxine had never skied before, but her friend had and assured Maxine that she would be skiing like a pro at the end of winter.

My imagination conjures up the following scenario as they see Alta and Little Cottonwood Canyon for the first time. Maxine and Anne's car wound up the curvy canyon with each woman lost in her own thoughts. What had they gotten themselves into? The mountains rose straight out of the canyon. It felt like they were in a giant ravine with steep avalanche chutes plunging dramatically down into the valley. Snow was swirling around them as if they had entered a child's Christmas snow globe. The road finally started to level out, and they saw the lights of the Alta Lodge. The only other sign of humanity were the humps of snow, which were recognizable as cars only because of their radio antennae sticking out. It was getting dark when they pulled their suitcases from the car and plowed through the fresh snow, which was over the tops of their boots to the door under the sign announcing Alta Lodge. When they stepped through the door, all they saw were many wooden steps leading downward, hopefully to the lodge. Giddy with excitement and the high altitude, they scampered down the ramp and finally found the front door after crossing a deck that extended all the way around the front of the lodge; luckily, it had been shoveled clear of snow. The door they entered was a big double wide painted deep red with large metal handles and a carved wooden sign announcing that, yes, indeed they had reached the Alta Lodge.

It was early November, and the lodge wasn't yet opened. When they plopped down their gear, they were standing near the front desk and took this moment to look around. The lobby was a large room, dominated by a red brick fireplace. The wooden furniture was situated around the fireplace and large picture windows. They could imagine how inviting it would be with a large fire crackling behind the mesh screen.

They could hear laughter coming from the dining room so, leaving their bags in the lobby, they went to find the rest of the crew. In the next hour, they had met most of the other employees and the assistant manager. They also had a tour of the lodge and discovered that they would be sleeping with other women in a dorm under the eaves of the roof, where there was a long line of beds with a bathroom at the end. Maxine was sure she left that kind of living behind when she graduated from college, but here she was again. Outside, it was still snowing and piling up fast as they unpacked and put on dry socks.

The lodge was due to open in a few days and, just as soon both girls would be waiting tables–breakfast, lunch and dinner–except on their days off.

Alta Lodge's rates were based on the European plan, which included room and three meals a day. So lodge guests always came in from skiing for lunch around the same time every day. The exception to this schedule was a really good powder day, when lunch was an afterthought to skiing.

In 1952, the lodge's rates for seven nights of lodging, 21 full meals, seven-day lift passes and seven lessons from the ski school, for a room with a connecting shower, was $85 per person. A dorm room was $7.20, which included three meals a day. Lift tickets alone were $2.75 a day. A blurb from the Alta Lodge brochure explained:

"The place to stay at Alta is The Alta Lodge, directly opposite the main ski lift. You put on your skis at the front door and ski down to the lift in a half a minute! The Lodge is small and its atmosphere is informal and friendly. There are open fireplaces in the lounge and club rooms, where picture windows bring the incomparable alpine scenery right to your chair. The Alta Lodge is recommended by Duncan Hines.

Some type of evening recreation is organized for the guest in Alta every night– movies, dance or folk dancing. There is a shop in The Lodge for ski repairs and rental equipment. Skiers' necessities also are available."

Maxine and her friend were quickly oriented to the dining room, kitchen and the chef, who was a challenge depending on his mood. If he felt great, the kitchen was a joy to work in. When the opposite was true, swinging through those double doors into the kitchen was an adventure full of danger, intrigue and often yelling. However, serving the guests was mostly a lot of fun. Evening meals were typically a set menu for each night of the week and so, besides serving the meal, they took drink orders and bussed the tables. Meals were served at a specific time, and everyone ate together. Meals were signaled by a bell rung by one of the waitresses through the halls of the lodge. After cleanup, the girls were on their own until the next morning for breakfast.

The Alta Lodge in those days was a family experience. Even those who were there alone felt part of the lodge family. In the evenings, the guests and employees would play cards, pool and ping-pong together. Employees also hung out with guests, and traveled during their brief time off to other lodges to see new faces and a different scene. When my mother arrived at the Alta Lodge there were, twelve to fourteen rooms, either with a bathroom down the hall or a connecting bath, plus a dorm for men and women.

After the lodge opened and the lifts were running for the season, Maxine began to practice her new skiing skills on the rope tow, or "bunny" hill, in front of the lodge. As many new skiers will tell you, the biggest challenge back then was learning to ride the rope tow and not just skiing down. The rope was heavy and, while you were struggling to hold on, you were still trying to keep your balance, your skis straight and stay up right. If someone fell, it usually pulled the rope down and to the side and, if the other skiers weren't prepared, they went down too. Getting off at the top involved letting go at the same time you stepped your skis sideways. The timing was very important. If you let go before you stepped, you slid backwards into the person behind you. The other scenario involved stepping before letting go, in which case, the rope flung back and knock off several other riders. Sometimes the skier's glove would be left twisted into the rope when the skier got off. Of course, the glove inadvertently fell off near the top wheel, where it was very hard to get. Often, leather gloves slipped on the snowy rope and skiers wouldn't move forward at all. Maxine learned early on to put one gloved hand behind her and one in front as she rode the tow.

Maxine was a cautious person and, after she had learned the snowplow and snowplow turn she slowly made her way down the "bunny" slope. Several ski instructors who frequented the lodge had given this attractive young woman pointers and watched out for her as she navigated on her skis. She was thrilled. As she became more skilled, she increased her speed and became more adventuresome. The next step was up the mountain on the chair lift.

The winter of 1949, Chic was working nights at the lodge bartending after working the lifts during the day. He had sold the stables and enjoyed the social aspect of bartending. He also was able to stay in the men's dorm and avoid the snowy drive down the steep canyon. As soon as the lodge opened, he found himself serving drinks and washing glasses in the Sitzmark Bar. Maxine was busy in the dining room in the early part of the evening, but later she would come for a drink to unwind before bed. It was hard not to notice the handsome young man behind the bar with startling blue eyes and a smile that stretched from one ear to the other. His curly brown hair was receding off his forehead but framed his tan face in a friendly invitation. As they got to know each other through the winter, their conversations would continue until logs in the fireplace burned to ash.

Chic and Maxine often walked the short distance to the Rustler Lodge and joined other friends, playing the guitar and singing on those long winter nights. Chic had a good voice and sang many love songs and cowboy ballads. Sverre Engen, Alf's brother and dear friend, was there with his guitar and often guests and employees would sing "Strawberry Roan," "Little Joe the Wrangler," way into the night, while the snow piled in drifts outside. Walking back arm in arm to the lodge at night the snow swirled around them, Chic and Maxine felt as if they were

Chic singing and Sverre Engen playing guitar at the Rustler Lodge

the only two people at Alta. The only beacon to let them know that they had reached the Alta lodge was the bright flood light above the sign; everything else was obscured by blowing snow. A good-night kiss outside the women's dorm was the ending of a romantic evening. Chic was up early working on the lifts while Maxine got up to get breakfast ready. They often would cross paths in the employee dining room before their busy days began. A few words over coffee were the most they would get until evening.

During those early days of their friendship/romance, little did they realize that- within the next few years-they would be ensconced at the lodge in a much deeper way and it would be the heartbeat of their lives for many years.

Maxine and Chic on the Germania Lift circa late 1950s

They had 18 years together as man and wife before Maxine died of cancer. Chic was devastated when Maxine died in 1968; he moved out of the Alta house and rented a small apartment in Salt Lake City. The only time he went back was when I came back for vacation from boarding school, in Carbondale, Colorado, for a visit. It was a sad time. He would call me at school and, often, we both would be–silent–just being with each other. I was the closest to him then when both of us were dealing with our pain in our own manner. When I came back that summer, we moved back into the house at Alta and tried to be a family again. I became the woman of the house and kept it clean, I cooked good meals, but I was only 14 and it was hard. Dad was always so appreciative of what I did for him. One day I had cleaned the kitchen before going off to do something with a friend. When I came back the kitchen was a mess because he had a friend for lunch. I remember yelling at him for the mess. He looked abashed and, after a few minutes and an apology, we both began laughing.

It wasn't until he married his second wife, Jean, that things were whole again. Chic and Jean married in April of 1970 in Las Vegas, Nevada, at the Chapel of Flowers. I and Jean's only daughter, Debbie Anderson, were with them on this festive occasion. Jean had been Chic's part-time administrative assistant after divorcing her first husband and was living in the Buckhorn when they started dating. I was thrilled to have Jean as a stepmother and best friend. For me, the stories of "ugly stepmothers" was truly a fable. She was a fabulous addition to our family she took good care of us loved adventure and was very supportive of Chic. Jean passed away after a bout with cancer. Her heart stopped beating in March of 2009.

Following a round of chemotherapy, Jean asked her doctor if she could go on an Africa safari before she had her next round. He agreed. She had a wonderful time and, even when she got sick again, all she could talk about were the wonderful animals in Africa.

CHAPTER #8

MEXICO AND MARRIAGE

That same winter, 1949, many feet of snow and thousands of turns later, the ski season had wound down. April is a fickle month in the mountains. It can be snowing one day and hot and sunny the next, but, by that time of year most everyone was ready for sun and green growing things. The Alta lodge served lunch on the deck so the guests could enjoy the mountain sun, watching skiers navigated High Rustler or swoop down Corkscrew, or giggling at snow bunnies who crashed on the rope tow hill. By spring that year, Maxine was skiing on the mountain but still liked easier runs on Germania, like Main Street or Mambo. Her turns were parallel now, and she enjoyed speed much more. As spring progressed and winter faded, she found herself sitting in the sun on the deck between her shifts rather than skiing, so it wasn't odd that, when Chic suggested a spring trip to Mexico with their friend Bob Card and his girlfriend, she was ready to go.

Bob had converted an old milk truck into a primitive motor home, and the four of them drove to Acapulco, where Maxine had a friend with a house. It was on this trip that Chic proposed marriage to Maxine. They both thought that they would settle in Salt Lake City and raise a family. Fate intervened again.

On the way back from Mexico, Chic put Maxine on a plane to Ohio in early May and didn't see her again until their wedding day at the end of December, in chilly Newark, Ohio. It was also the first time he met his in-laws. Chic loved to tell the story of walking up the driveway to the Norpell house that first time with his knees knocking together because he was so nervous. He hadn't seen Maxine for almost seven months, and questions flew through his mind. Would she be the same? Would her parents like him? Was the ring he bought too simple? It seemed like the longest driveway in the world to him at that moment. A simple white house sat in front of him, surrounded with snow. It was late in the day, and golden pools of light puddled on the snow. The porch light glowed like a beacon to a lost sailor. Maxine must have been watching for him because she threw open the door as he climbed the steps and suddenly all his questions didn't matter for there stood the woman he loved, smiling and mirroring the adoration he felt.

Chic and Maxine's wedding December 30, 1950

The wedding was small with only immediate family invited. It was held in the home of Max Norpells. Both of Maxine's brothers were there as well as brother Tim's wife, Press, and, of course, Maxine's parents—Dorothy and Max. Chic was only there for a few days, and Dorothy waited to have the ceremony until the day before they had to leave for the long drive back to Salt Lake City and their new life together. Their first night out on the road–their honeymoon–Chic found a bottle of champagne which Tim had snuck into the back seat of the car. There was no time for much more of a honeymoon because Chic had to get back to work, having used up his vacation driving the long distance, 1834 miles, to Ohio and then home.

Chic had taken a real job with a frozen food company and rented a nice apartment for them in Salt Lake City. Once again, what they thought of as their new life would take a drastic turn in a different direction. When Fred Speyer came by the apartment one evening and asked them if they would like to be the new managers at the lodge, they took only moments to decide. So much for conventional married life. Now, instead of ski bums, they were in charge of all the employees and the operation of the lodge. Instead of living in the dorm, they had a tiny apartment in the basement of the lodge under the very porch in which Maxine and her friend Anne had arrived on the winter before.

Life for the newly married couple was busy and chaotic. They both loved the social aspect of their jobs but were always challenged by managing employees, schedules, guest reservations and finances. Chic often said that this was the happiest time in his life. He was a born host and, if truth be told, I think he enjoyed the challenges of keeping the lodge running on a daily basis. Maxine was also a gracious hostess and, keeping the front desk and reservations running smoothly plus the maids and the dining room staff was plenty to keep her busy.

When speaking of his time at Alta and the lodge, Chic said, "I have always thought it was the best thing that happened to me because I enjoyed every minute of it."

There were plenty of challenges with old plumbing in the lodge, days of no inter-lodge travel with lodge guests trapped in the lodge and no supplies coming in, employee issues, avalanches, raising a child, working long hours, seven days a week, and a myriad of other events that made life interesting. Not to mention, the lodge made most of its money during the winter holidays when the lodge was full. There was very little downtime from November through April. The interesting conversations with guests not only were their social outlet but a relaxing time for them both.

Maxine was a social creature and found people who visited the lodge a delight and source of constant stimulation. My memories of my parents during this time were full of laughter, fun and long hours. It wasn't uncommon for me to look up from playing with one of my many stuffed animals to see the two of them wrapped in a hug and staring into each others faces with a look of pure contentment. Though I wouldn't recognize this look as the deep and committed love it was until I was much older, I could feel the warmth and security that love created for me.

In the early 1950s, while Chic and Maxine were busy making Alta Lodge a memorable place to stay, the ski world was popping. More than 1,000 rope tows had sprung up in North America's snowy mountains. Only 78 of the ski areas actually had wire-cable lifts, either with chair lifts, pomas or T-bars. Several bigger resorts, like Alta, offered lodges and on-mountain restaurants, but many offered only the basic ski experience. Skiers were still traveling to Europe for the full package ski vacation. Things changed fast when ski lifts replaced rope tows, and slope grooming and snow making arrived, giving the North American ski areas a boost over, the Europeans. It also was the time when the first metal ski became available and helped change the sport. Those first skis were called Head skis after the inventor Howard Head. I remember my first pair of Head skis were hand-me-downs called the Standard Head Ski. They were black with tiny yellow lettering on them, announcing the manufacturer and model. They were claimed to be a cheater ski because they were so easy to ski on. The price for those skis in the early 1950s was $85. Not too long after that came buckle boots and release bindings that saved many skiers from broken legs and bad sprains.

Ski clothes up to this time were considered for function only. Then, in 1952 Maria Bogner from Munich, designed the stretch pant. These pants not only flattered the wearer, they felt sleek and fast. Stretch pants stayed in fashion until the 1980s when the snowboard influence brought back baggy pants.

CHAPTER #9

SNOWED IN

When the snow fell in Little Cottonwood Canyon, it didn't fool around. The clouds would build, thicken and lower as they picked up moisture over the Great Salt Lake and, when they hit the mountains, they dumped millions and millions of dry white crystals. Snow accumulates quickly when it snows an inch or two an hour. Snowstorms of my childhood, as well as Chic and Maxine's early years at Alta, always came in many feet. Those feet of snow changed the character of the landscape drastically. Not only were cars buried, but most of the buildings were smothered in thick white snow. What once were creek beds, ravines and large boulders sprinkled across the mountain sides now were nothing but feet and feet of snow. Branches of spruce trees were pillowed with fresh snow, and their lower branches buried until late spring. Creeks and rivers froze over and disappeared. As the snow depth increased, the trees both aspen and spruce– became shorter and shorter with many of them disappearing all together.

Little Cottonwood Canyon's only road is nine miles long with Salt Lake City at 4,500 feet and the base of Alta at 8,000 feet above sea level. Take a moment and do the math: 3,500 feet of elevation gain in nine miles. Let's just say that driving down that canyon feels more like a drop than a casual cruise. The mountains on either side of this steep canyon rise straight up. Once in Alta proper, the valley floor flattens and opens up but the mountains still rise radically out of the bottom. As more and more snow falls over the winter, the snow piles up on these mountains. Result: weight gets to be too much and the snow moves. Snow in mass, especially when it is moving, weighs plenty and has a lot of power. AVALANCHE!

Early on, in order to keep skiers, residents, cars and businesses safe the U.S. Forest Service started a snow safety program. This amounted to working with the highway department to close the road when they deemed it unsafe, shutting down the foot and vehicle traffic between all buildings at Alta and closing the ski mountain. This situation, was called interlodge closure, could last for hours or days and the same thing held true for the road. When a storm moved out, they would "shoot" down the avalanches by pelting the slopes with World War II Howitzer guns.

In 1965, it snowed and snowed and snowed. The avalanche danger was high. They closed the roads, warning out of town guests to get out while they could. Many guests stayed, hoping for some outrageous powder skiing when the storm cleared. The Forest Service declared it dangerous not only to ski but also to move from building to building, so interlodge closed as well as the ski lifts. The snow kept falling.

As I write these recollections, I am looking out on a snowy day, probably half an inch an hour accumulates. The deep green of the ponderosa pines gives contrast to the white sky, white snow and white ground. At Alta, this is not true because Alta's trees were cut during the mining years for timbers, homes and businesses; trees were no longer in abundance. The point is that, looking out the windows of the Alta Lodge, all one saw was white. When it is snowing that hard, whiteness covers everything quickly and there is no contrast. The lodge guests soon found that the novelty of being "trapped" wore off and they got true "cabin fever". A forced relaxation at first is a treat but can quickly become boring. There were books to read, board games, including chess and checkers, a pool and ping-pong table. I'm sure hours were consumed with conversation and debate on current events and politics, AND still there was time left over. Chic and Maxine helped as much as they could to keep the guests and employees sane.

After breakfast one morning, Chic announced that, in order to get into the dining room that night, each guest had to make a unique hat and compete for a prize given to the most creative one. During the day, a table was set up with magic markers, colored pencils, paper bags, ribbon, wrapping paper and other things for creative minds to work with. The employees were not exempt, and both guests and employees spent the entire day absorbed in this project. When dinner-time arrived, a variety of "hats" adorned the dining room accompanied by much laughter and explanations.

Another evening, guests served food to employees and dressed in costume to add more entertainment. The lodge attracted all kinds of people—from owners of major corporations to ski bums but, here at the lodge and in these circumstances, everyone was at the same level. The entertainment value was immense for all involved.

In the evenings, Chic would roll back the rugs, bring out his guitar or Alf Engen, the ski school director, would bring his accordion and soon there would be singing and dancing. I spent many an evening standing on my father's shoes trying to learn to polka. During this particular interlodge closure, anyone who could play an instrument or sing was brought forward. There was an abundance of laughter and time melted away, unlike the many feet of snow outside.

Being bored was a problem, but feeding all those people with no new supplies coming in was a challenge. I know that, at least once when the storm let up for a few hours several snow-cats traveled down the canyon to take guests out and bring in supplies. The chef also had to be creative in his cooking and pay attention to his supplies to keep everyone fed. When the storms finally ended and the sun came out, the Forest Service had to "encourage" the avalanches to come down before they slid unexpectedly. So, they started to shoot with big military guns. It sounded much like a war zone though there really wasn't an enemy–just winter doing its thing.

CHAPTER 10

FAMILY LIFE

The lodge took all of Chic and Maxine's spare time in the winter but, in the summers after the lodge was closed, it was empty, gloomy and lonely. Maxine longed for a home of her own. The summer after I was born, Chic and Maxine hiked around Alta looking for a place to build. Of course they wanted a view down the canyon and of Devil's Castle, Sugarloaf and Superior Mountains. They also wanted good water and good summer road access.

I was born in April 1954, and was a surprise because my mother wasn't sure she could have children due to health issues. So, when I came into the world on a snowy April day, they were more determined than ever to have their own home. Chic told the story of driving Maxine to the hospital when she was in labor while he looked up at Mt. Superior Mountain and saw a wet snow avalanche starting up high on the mountain. He was sure he could beat it, it was moving so slowly. He didn't mention it to Maxine but stepped on the gas and roared down the road under that slide path. Maxine just assumed he thought the baby was coming and tried to reassure him that being alive was as important as having the baby early. The slide did cover the road behind them, and I was safely delivered in Holy Cross Hospital in Salt Lake City.

Dealing with a baby who quickly became a small child in the lodge, was a challenge for them. In our first apartment under the deck, we didn't have a private bathroom. We shared it with the assistant manager. The bathroom had only a shower, any baths occurred in the old ringer washing machine in the hall. The big tub was a perfect fit for a small child, and Maxine could even stand while she bathed me. The only issue I had with this arrangement was the fact the washing machine was in a public place. Also, we didn't have our own kitchen in our apartment, so all the preparation and feeding of an infant and subsequent small child was done in the commercial kitchen. Imagine preparing baby bottles and, baby food in a kitchen where every pot, pan and appliances was designed to feed 20 or more people.

Maxine was active in the management of the lodge and also was a mother. She used a playpen in the office and behind the front desk but when I got bigger, I'm sure her challenges grew. I do remember having a harness and a leash much like they use to teach small children to ski.

The lodge was a great playground for a small child but also had many dangers. There were stairs everywhere, fireplaces in the lobby and bar, plus a large kitchen with cooks and waitresses to get tangled up with. The employees were also my caretakers, and I am sure I added another dimension to their jobs. My parents were host and hostess every night of the week. They would spend early evenings in the lodge bar, called the Sitzmark, and then went to dinner with the guests when the bell rang. I ate earlier and spent the evening in our apartment playing.

So they were thrilled when, in the summer of 1955, they found the perfect spot for a house. They had been hiking with me on their backs looking for most of the summer. It was a mining claim called Patsy Marley's Petticoat that was owned by United Mining Company. They bought a large chunk of land and then sold off several lots in order to have money enough to build our house. It was a barren place with big boulders and not much vegetation. The footers and foundation went in with help from the Nichols family. Chic and Maxine built a simple mountain house made of green cinder blocks with huge picture windows and outrageous views of Alta Valley, down the canyon and up into Albion Basin. There were two stone fireplaces–one upstairs and one in the basement– that were well built so that they kept the house toasty even when the power was off. A porch ran around two sides of the house for summer viewing of the mountains.

By winter 1955, the house was dried in but not livable, though the carpenters stayed in it and worked on the inside. I have heard bits and pieces of the story that the carpenters spent more time skiing than working on the house, but nonetheless, in the summer of 1956, we left the lodge and moved into our own little home on the hill. We lived in our new house summers only until Dad sold the lodge in 1965, and then we moved into the house fulltime while Dad worked for the lift company year round as his only job.

Living at the house in the winter entailed many challenges. The biggest one was that the road to the house was unplowed from November through April, which is why we used snow machines for our transportation. It meant that, like squirrels, we needed to store up food for the winter. Mom, and then later my stepmother Jean, typically spent the fall caching canned goods and frozen things in the freezer. Our goal was to buy only fresh things on our weekly trip to Salt Lake City like milk, eggs, fruit and vegetables, which were easier to transport the mile to the house. In reverse we had to dispose of household garbage. Our house had an incinerator to burn paper trash. We washed and smashed all the cans and bottles to be disposed of in the spring. This was long before recycling was available. The "wet" garbage was kept separate and carried to town on our

Morton's Alta house in midwinter

once weekly trip. We had three trash containers under the sink for each type of trash. It was interesting trying to explain our complicated system to my school friends who lived

in the city. When Mom or Jean and I went to town, we either rode in the cat to where our cars were parked at the end of the plowed road or walked down the track left by the snowcat. When I was in high school and drove myself to school, I walked to the car most mornings and home in the afternoons. On really snowy days, Dad would take me to the car in our snowcat and help me dig out. When we left the house, we wore snow boots and winter clothes but when we got to the cars, we changed for school or town activities. When summer finally arrived in Alta in late June or July, we could finally drive to our house, which was considered a great treat.

Unlike many ski towns, Alta had no commercial facilities–no grocery store, gas station or any other stores except for ski stuff. Salt Lake City was the closest place for shopping. Though it was only nine miles away, on a day when it was storming, it was a very long nine miles.

After the Morton house sprang up, other lot owners built their own homes. Next door, Baldy built a cozy little house, and then the Matzingers–Merrell and Alisha–built a home below us, using our basic floor plan but adding a garage and a bit more square footage. The Simons built the house below us, using a design that made it look like a Swiss chalet. To this day, the owners have kept that unique style while modernizing it. Each of our neighbors bought a small Tucker snowcat. The cab only held one person so a trailer was towed behind for groceries and luggage. I remember that Baldy's wife, Sue, painted a duck on the door of his machine. My family used a war surplus Army weasel. It was a functional vehicle that looked like a tank with the top cut off. There were bench seats in the back, and the driver sat up front it was open to the air. All of the over-the- snow machines in those days were mechanical, with no hydraulics like they have now. But they did the trick and moved over the deep snow and up the steep hills surrounding the houses with ease. After we moved fulltime into our house, I would listen for the sound of Dad's small snowcat moving along the valley floor as he drove home from the lift building. That sound is still comforting to me.

Maxine became very adept at driving the weasel which, for some odd reason we never named, and puttered back and forth between the lodge and house. One winter day, we had come up to the house in the morning to get it ready for some of Maxine's friends who were coming for lunch. After our preparations, Maxine left to drive down and pick up the gals. The main route down to the lodge, which Chic had created early in the winter without following the summer road but instead, plunging steeply down in front of the house, was the one Maxine took. Maxine had tried shifting to a lower gear as she was plummeting down that hill. Along with a finicky clutch and too much speed, she got stuck in neutral. Between the speed and her fear of being out of control, she ended up tipping the weasel over in a large tree well. As a small child, I watched the whole thing from the porch and was equally frightened and crying. Maxine was not hurt and climbed out of the machine. She yelled to me to call Chic. I obliged with much sniffing. After that, lunch went on without a hitch as Chic picked up the guests and got some of the lift guys to help right the snow machine. Just another day in the lives of mountain dwellers!

I was a teenager when Dad encouraged and taught me to drive the small Thiokol snowcat, called an Imp, which he had upgraded to after the weasel and several lodge cats, and I was thrilled. I only had one incident, and he was in the cat with me. We were driving down to the place the cars were parked at the end of the road (actually the end of the plowed road), and it was flat light in a snowstorm when I got one track off the road, the cat flipped over on its side. I had a similar experience learning to drive a truck and flipped it on its side, too. Both times, Dad was with me. I must have gotten it out of my system because since then I have stayed upright in every vehicle I have driven. Chic was patient in teaching me to drive, and I still hear his advice in my head. I was a cautious child and, when I was learning something new, I felt insecure. He always encouraged me but didn't always hear the real fear in my voice, which is why both vehicles ended up on their sides.

Our home, perched on the side of the mountain, was comfortable and private. We lived there every summer after it was finished and often, before we left the lodge, came up in the winter to get away from the chaos of lodge living. In fact, every Christmas we would try to spend Christmas Eve and morning at the house to have some family time. That only happened if the toilets didn't clog, the chef didn't quit or the moody furnace didn't act up.

During those years at the lodge, Maxine and Chic often entertained at the house. It was a treat for the lodge guests to ski or be brought up in the snowcat for an evening of appetizers and cocktails. The guests would stand around sipping drinks and munching snacks while watching the sun slip westward and the mountains turn the crimson of alpenglow. One of the frequent guests to these parties was Lowell Thomas, a famous newscaster and a world traveler, who was a great story teller. Chic was also an avid story teller and could make the most mundane incident seem exciting. He often told his stories at these cocktail parties and the lodge bar.

Chic was strict as a father but mostly fair. When I was a teenager and wanted more freedom, he was willing for me to explore the world on my own. He often told me that he trusted me and knew I wouldn't break the rules of our family. Both my cousin Annette and I would do almost anything not to have him give us the "disappointed Chic" look and tell us that we had let him down. I'm not saying that we didn't get into trouble, because we did after all, it was inevitable for teenagers.

For example, one summer evening in early 1970s there was a party at the Alpenglow Restaurant, located in the Albion Basin above Alta. The Alpenglow was home to the Walker family, where they lived with five kids, four boys and a girl so their parties included kids. This particular night, the adults were imbibing and having a grand time and had begun to sing as the sun was setting. We were soon bored and took off on an evening walk, forgetting to mention our departure to any of the adults. I know that we didn't have a destination in mind when we wandered off but, as we clambered up the mountainside, we realized how close we were to one of our favorite haunts–Cecret Lake, (the spelling is either because the miner who had the Cecret mining claim couldn't spell or he just liked the correct spelling). The lake was about two miles from the Alpenglow, and it took us less than an hour to get there. There was still enough light to see the reflection of Sugarloaf Mountain in the lake, though the scenery wasn't as interesting to us as throwing rocks in the lake and, for Annette and me to flirt with two of the Walker boys–Tom and Andy.

We had settled ourselves on some rocks by the lake and noticed it was getting pretty dark. It still hadn't occurred to us that we would soon be missed from the party because we were having too much fun. It wasn't long before we noticed that there were headlights of several trucks driving up the summer access road on Greeley Hill, which was directly above the Alpenglow and in our line of sight.

I do believe that it occurred to all of us about the same time that those trucks were probably looking for us. At some point in the evening, the adults must have realized that the children were gone. I imagine them laughing and then calling and then getting a bit frantic and then mad. After all, we were in our early teens and obviously not very responsible.

In a bit of a panic, we bolted down the trail as fast as we could and met up with some anxious and angry parents on the deck of the Alpenglow. By this time, the trucks on the mountain had turned around and their headlights were bouncing down the mountain.

Nothing much was said until we got home, when Annette and I both got the disappointed looks and "the speech".

When I was in high school I chose to stay at home on several weekends when Chic and Jean went off. I was told: absolutely no parties or overnight male guests. Annette and I had several friends for dinner and, when we told them they had to go home, they were amazed that we were so "afraid" of my Dad. It was difficult to explain to them that it wasn't fear but the need to have his respect that kept us from breaking the rules.

The flip sides were on the rare occasions when Dad told me he was proud of me; it meant the world to me. He was not one to give compliments easily but, when they came, they were heartfelt by both giver and receiver.

Because Chic set such high standards for himself and those who worked for him, he also encouraged those same standards for me. I often felt I couldn't quite measure up. When I would get frustrated about my performance, he would often remind me that doing the best we can is enough. And this would take some of the pressure off me.

Chic was not a religious man in the sense that he didn't attend church of a formal religion. From my perspective, he was a deeply spiritual man. My mother would take me to church on

Sundays in the summer while Chic would stay home. At age nine, after thinking things over for awhile, I told Mom I didn't want to go to church any more. In her gentle and wise manner, she respected my wishes. Later, Dad and I were sitting on the porch and he asked me why I didn't want to go to church any more. I said quite simply: "God doesn't live in church." Chic got one of his famous grins on his face and asked me, "So, where does God live, Kim?" "Right here in these mountains, Daddy." And then, after a little pause I asked, "Don't you think so?" Chic chuckled and put his arm around my shoulders and, looking at the scenery around us, said, "Yes, Kim, I think he does."

Both my father and I found great spiritual comfort wandering around in the mountains, discovering, both peace and understanding about a confusing and often violent world. I love the fact that his ashes are still under the tree where our house once stood and he can look forever out on his beloved Alta.

When my Dad was growing up in Salt Lake City during the 1920s the dominant religion was The Latter Day Saints (LDS) or the Mormon religion. The Mortons were not Mormons, but Chic had a lot of respect for many aspects of the religion. He admired their connection to family and how they took such good care of other members of their church. By the time I started in public school in 1961, I was one of two children in my elementary school who was not Mormon. With those numbers, most of my friends were Mormon. I found that if I wanted to spend time with my best friend, Sue Green, I would have to attend Primary, which was an after-school religious class. I didn't last very long because I kept asking questions which many of the teachers couldn't answer. Neither Chic nor Maxine had a problem with my taking part in other religious traditions.

Like many men of his time, Chic kept several rifles in a locked gun case in our home. He had a shotgun for hunting birds, a big gun for deer hunting, and .22-caliber rifle for smaller game. He hunted for meat only. Being a curious young girl, I asked lots of questions about the guns and Dad's hunting. I'm not too sure that my mother, Maxine, was too thrilled but he taught me to shoot the .22 and all the safety issues that went with firing a gun. He would set up cans on the porch, and I would shoot them off the railing. I was a good aim and did well.

One early summer day when the leaves were still bright green on the trees and nights had a bite to them, Dad took me out to hunt rabbits. He wanted me to experience what hunting a wild animal entailed. After tromping around for a short while, a snowshoe rabbit that had turned back to his summer brown dashed out of the spruce trees. Chic was on it and shot the animal. I remember being a bit surprised at how sad I felt when this creature fell dead. Part of the lesson was about preparing and cleaning the animal for eating, so I helped in the entire process. As we opened her up, she was carrying babies. It broke both our hearts, and we both cried at the sight. We decided we would bury the rabbit instead of eating her. Neither of us could think of cooking her. I know that Chic still hunted after that incident and brought home ducks, pheasants and deer for our freezer. I wasn't as enthusiastic about hunting myself and, when I went along it was not to hunt.

When I was married to my first husband, who was a hunter, we invited Chic to come elk hunting with us in the mountains north of Durango, Colorado. Utah doesn't have the abundance of elk that we have in Colorado so he was thrilled. We decided to hire wranglers and horses to take us in, set up a camp and then come and take us out at the end of the hunt. At this point, early 1980s, it had been years since Chic had been on a horse. We loaded ourselves and our gear on the horses and off we went up a winding mountain trail. Two of my husband's friends went with us; I was there to be the camp cook. The horses we had were exhausted from too many other "drop camps", and we had a few incidents on the way into our camp. One pack horse rolled off the trail and, fortunately, we had only minor damage. My horse tried to roll with me on her. I quickly, jumped out of the way. Chic was having a bit of problem sitting in the saddle because his hips were stiff. When the wrangler said something about being an old man, I got incensed and lit into him, defending my father's riding ability. Chic chuckled when he heard me sticking up for him. The wrangler's comments didn't bother him in the least.

We set up our camp on a large basin just below timberline. It was a lovely fall day, warm and dry, and we set up a large wall tent and an outdoor kitchen. We spent the afternoon "scouting" for elk, which in my mind meant a time to walk around and explore where we were.

Hunting season started the next morning. My agreement with the men was that they could make their own coffee and have a few snacks before dawn and then, when they got back mid-morning, I would make them a full-fledged breakfast. So, I was safely snuggled in my sleeping bag when the men went off that morning. About dawn, I was sure we were in a war zone. I have never heard so many guns going off. Being curious, I got up and peeked outside the tent as a herd of ten elk ran right through our camp. I dove back into my bag, afraid someone would start shooting at the elk and hit me by mistake. Moments later, my husband ran through camp and shot a cow elk. I found it wasn't any easier to see her die than it was seeing the rabbit die many years earlier.

 Chic was hunting a bit higher in the valley and, while the elk was being gutted, I went to find him. He was sitting perched behind a rock with his rifle lying on the stone, looking peaceful and content. I sat down beside him and told him about John's elk and how sad I felt. He proceeded to share with me that, for him, the fun of hunting was wandering around the mountains and seeing the magnificent animals as they grazed or ran in their own environment. He said that the work really began after the animal hit the ground. The gutting, quartering and hauling were tough. He smiled a lazy smile and, as we watched, a herd of elk meandered through the meadow below us. I was in awe of their beauty and saw Chic smile and nod. His gun never moved. That moment with my Dad and those elk will stay with me forever. We were all creatures of those mountains, and nothing was going to die from Chic's gun that day.

We woke the next morning to almost two feet of fresh snow. I made a wonderful breakfast of bacon, eggs, blueberry muffins and coffee and then walked the eight miles out to the car because I had to go to work the next day. They shot another elk before the hunt was over but Chic's rifle stayed quiet. That trip, in early October, 1982, was the last of Chic's hunting.

Entangled in Chic and Maxine's hectic life at the lodge was getting me to school and home. The school bus was not allowed to enter Little Cottonwood Canyon so someone had to drive me to the mouth of the canyon, where I picked up a small bus that took me to a big bus that took me to school. Sometimes the handyman at the lodge would take me down, sometimes my Dad; when the roads were good, often Mom would drive. It wasn't unusual for everyone to get busy and either forget to pick me up or be late. Mom arranged for me to go to a friend's house at the mouth of the canyon when that happened. It was always an adventure getting to school and home again. I only remember sliding off the road once, but there were some scary drives down that canyon. I think everyone breathed a sigh of relief when all I had to do was walk across the road and up the hill to school during the winter months with Dolores when she tutored Randy and me at the upper guard station.

My parents knew that getting me to school would be a challenge so Mom tried to home-school me in first grade. It wasn't a big success for either of us. Starting second grade, I commuted every morning and evening. After Christmas break, when Ed LaChapelle, the head snow ranger, had arrived with his wife, Dolores, and son, Randy, Dolores would teach both of us in the upper guard station. Randy was a year ahead of me in school but, since we were the only two kids, it worked well. We continued this way until April, when the ski area closed and the LaChapelles went back to Washington for the summer. Then back I went to commuting twice a day. Everyone was very glad when I finally was able to drive myself.

Part of who we were as a family was the fact that my father and I shared in the untimely death of my mother and his wife, Maxine. It taught us how fleeting life could be, how important each day was with those we love and about not taking anything for granted. Chic believed life was all about lessons learned and what you did with those lessons. A very practical life lesson that Chic taught me was that, if you owned your own home, you could weather almost any life crisis. He used the example of my mother's illness.

When my mother, Maxine, experienced her first bout of cancer I was five. She had a radical mastectomy, and doctors told her then that they may not have gotten all the cancer cells. It was then they informed her that she probably had only ten years to live. After this first illness the insurance company canceled her insurance. When her cancer came back, Chic had to mortgage the house to by the hospital bills. Luckily, he owned our home.

A family remains a family even if one or more of the members are gone. We never stopped missing Mom and we knew the importance of being open to someone new being a mom and a wife. We were so lucky when Jean found our family.

The Morton Family enjoying summer at the Alta house, 1963

CHAPTER 11

THE ALTA LODGE

The Alta Lodge was our home, our business and an inviting place for Alta folks to stay and work.

As I remember Alta Lodge, it had a charming alpine ambiance. Wood-burning fireplaces both in the lobby and bar, wood paneling, and knotty wood furniture with leather cushions made for a cozy place to socialize, read or watch the snow fall.

Large windows offered stunning views to the south and west. Mt. Superior dominated the southern view, with its massive slopes and rocky cliffs. The west windows looked up the Collins Lift to Mt. Baldy, where the famous Baldy chutes plunged down its face into a gentle bowl called Ballroom. High Rustler, Alta's signature ski run, flared its snowy face down to the flats below the lodge. The top of the run is no wider than a couple of ski lengths bordered by spindly high altitude trees and, by the time a skier has hit the bottom, it is well over one-quarter mile wide. These views assured that it was never boring looking out those windows.

On a fiercely snowy day, the sight out the windows showed blowing snow swirling and trying to land all was white and, in early evenings, the sun would glow magenta on the mountains–alpenglow. The early morning light on the mountains would blush with an orange gleam and, as the days drew to a close, sunsets would settle over the Salt Lake Valley, creating an awesome light show of orange and magenta. On the nights when the moon was growing full, its cool light would bounce off the snow and make it look almost like day. When the moon was dark, the stars were so vivid and close that it felt as if my head was touching them when I walked outside.

The bar, or as it was called, "The Sitzmark Club" was upstairs under the eaves of the lodge, with dormer windows looking to the west. This name originated from the German word sitzmark, which was the hole skiers made when they fell in the snow. It was not uncommon to see a sign near the top of the lift encouraging skiers to "please fill in their sitzmarks".

Large picture windows on either side of the fireplace looked out on High Rustler and the ski runs serviced by Collins Lift. Couches snuggled under the eaves, and small bar tables with rustic wood chairs were scattered about. In front of the fireplace were a couch and a long table where a game of chess was often in progress. The bar itself was on the north wall and, opposite that, a cozy booth held more than a few couples who would steal kisses in its dark recess.

As kids, we were not allowed in the bar and, being mischievous, we found that we could sneak in the door and scurry behind the couch to listen to the adults talk. We found it quite boring and only stayed a short time but the fun of being in the forbidden bar was the real treat. We were allowed to go to the back door of the bar and ask for a soda or a Shirley Temple, but the bar was for adults.

Rooms in the old section of the lodge were generic with beds, sinks, dressers and a shared bathroom. The knotty pine paneling gave rooms the warm glow of wood, and the colorful bedspreads and curtains added a vibrant touch. Each room had a small window that let in natural light and helped make the rooms seem a bit bigger than they actually were. I am not sure where the origin of this tradition started but the maids always left a basket on the dresser of each room with peanuts, oranges and apples in it. As I look back, I can't imagine the mess those peanut shells must have made on the floors.

The dorms were upstairs under the eaves. In the early days, they were for the guests and later, when the new wing was built they were used for employees. The women's dorm was on one end the men's on the other. There also was a guest suite on that floor called the Swiss Room. It was much larger than all the other rooms with a couch and comfortable chairs in a sitting area as well as beds and a private bath. Behind the bar, there were rooms for employees but, at the very end of the hall, was another guest room called the Ship's Cabin. It had a double bed built into the wall and enough room for a dresser and a sink, but that was it. It always seemed as if only rich, single men stayed there. There was a bit of a mystery surrounding that room, probably directly related to the interesting guests who slept there.

The basement housed more employee quarters and another guest suite on the opposite side as the employees it was very spacious and could fit an entire family. I remember that the

Leavitt family used this when they came to stay. It was called the Tyrolean Room. The second floor also had a dorm area with bunk beds and bathrooms down the hall where many of the single guests stayed and later, as they needed more rooms for employees, this became theirs.

In the basement, besides employee quarters and the guest suite, was the furnace room, the old coal room turned into pool table room, the liquor store (state-owned) along with apartments for us and the assistant manager. The larger main space had ski lockers and a waxing bench plus a ping-pong table.

Often people who were skiing on the Alta Lodge rope tow would come and use the pit toilets that were tucked away in a corner of the basement. One of my memories of living at the lodge as a child is going to sleep listening to the ping-pong ball being batted back and forth across the table and the smell of hot ski wax permeating the air.

Chic spent many hours roaming all these spaces in the lodge. Every evening before he retired, he walked all the halls and turned down the thermostats. He checked the kitchen, the front desk; he made sure that the screens were in front of both fireplaces and finally the furnace before he went to bed. At five every morning, he did the same routine in reverse. The lodge had a handyman who could cleverly fix almost anything, but Chic was there behind him with a helping hand. It was not unusual to see Chic with either a shovel, a toilet plunger or a screwdriver in his hand. Maxine's tools of choice were the adding machine, a pencil and the phone.

My step-mother, Jean, always said about my father that he was a natural host and storyteller. He loved his work at the lodge and, even with the long hours and stress, he enjoyed the challenges and the people. We both felt he would've loved to stay there forever running the lodge but fate had another direction for him.

Chic and Maxine started managing the lodge in 1951 and, in 1958, Fred Speyer asked Chic to manage the lift company as well as the lodge. Fred was having some health problems and needed to get out of the cold and high altitude.

So for over ten years, Chic had a finger in a couple of the Alta pies and enjoyed them both. Buck Sasaki was the lift guru who kept those lifts operating and managed employees to run them. Chic also had an assistant manager of the lodge who helped Maxine and him keep the gears in motion necessary to operate a guest lodge, feed people three meals, manage the employees and keep the accounting aspect straight. The lodge was a seven-day-a-week, 24-hour, per day job. New guests came on Saturdays and left the next Saturday. It was always a busy place, especially during the holidays when all the rooms were full.

As both the ski area company grew and the lodge outgrew its few rooms, Chic needed a partner. So Bill Leavitt entered the picture. With his investment, they were able to build a new wing the lodge and more rooms. Until 1968, Chic and Maxine juggled many balls–the lodge, the lifts and family. Chic sold his shares of the lodge to Bill when it became obvious that they had differences in business philosophy which had become too apparent to ignore.

Alta Lodge with the new wing.

I know that Dad missed the lodge tremendously; I think Maxine was happy and ready to have a simpler life, especially in the winter. However, when she left the lodge, she found she had the challenge of keeping her social life active, so she skied with friends, played bridge, and she and Dad often went to the lodges for dinner with guests and friends. In the summer, she played tennis and hiked with the many friends she had acquired since moving to Alta.

The Alta Lodge was a magical place, especially to a young child. There was a warm feel about the place that I attribute to the fun people who worked there, the lodge guests, the cozy fireplaces burning on cold and snowy days, the aroma of fresh baked goods coming from the kitchen, and the merry laughter of skiers after many great powder turns. The bar and lobby danced with the spirits of all the guests who had ever stayed at the lodge.

On a typical snowy Saturday evening after the dining room had cleared of guests, Svere and Alf Engen often would be found in the lobby with their accordion and guitar as Chic rolled back the rugs for dancing. Soon the knotty pine walls of the lobby would be resounding with music, and the floors were vibrating with dancing feet. The snow outside was falling, and occasionally, a gust of wind would send the flakes swirling and twirling, to land and pile up quickly, covering everything with a white mantel. After a few hours of dancing, guests would retire early to be rested for the new powder snow in the morning.

When the next morning dawned clear and cold and the mountains glistened with new snow, amazingly all that white stuff created a new danger of avalanche and it would take some time to get the road and mountain open.

So the guests lingered over their coffee in the dining room as they listened to the guns shoot down avalanches. From one view in the dining room, birds were competing for goodies at the feeder. Stellar jays, grey jays, and chickadees were rivaling for their share. A squirrel, sitting in a nearby tree, squawked his displeasure at having to wait for the larger birds to leave. Waitresses dressed in colorful uniforms cheerfully greeted guests and refilled their coffee cups.

The tables were set up for intimate groups of four or larger sets of eight to ten. The conversation was eclectic, with people from all over the country and all different backgrounds, educations and occupations. Alta Lodge was a natural equalizer all the guest were here for the same thing—skiing Alta's famous light and dry powder snow.

A gust of cold air entered the lobby as Ed LaChapelle, Alta's snow ranger came in and shook the snow off his coat. The guests queried him about when the mountain would be open. Ed laughed good naturally and answered all their questions.

The chef, Bob, waddled out of the kitchen and greeted the guests. He plopped his abundant body in a chair, his clothes smelling of grease, sweat and good food. He was often a bear to the waitresses but a delight to the guests who enjoyed his cooking. He asked Ed when the road would be open so he could get in some fresh supplies.

Several hours later, the lifts opened and the guests grabbed their skis from lockers in the basement, laughing and excited to get skiing. A few skiers were still waxing their skis, and the smell of Alf Engen's ski wax followed the skiers out the door. At lunch they were all back in with great stories to tell of their adventures and some down time to take off their boots and rest before more turns in the afternoon.

Christmas-time was a magical event at Alta Lodge. Chic started off the holiday season's cheer with a tree-cutting party.

Picture this scene: as snow fell in a solid curtain of white, large, soft flakes covered everything in a gentle blanket. Etched across the snow were the gentle arcs left by skiers on the crystalline surface. The soft winter light faded as guests from Alta Lodge gathered in Albion Basin for the annual tree-cutting party.

A bonfire and plus tables of finger food and hot drinks greeted guests as they skied up and stuck their skis in the snow. Chic held a saw in one hand and, with his other, he gripped the trunk of a large tree that he had climbed halfway. Other guests stood close to the fire, snacking on goodies. Chic yelled "timber" right before the top of the tree fell with a plop in the deep snow. Cutting only the top of the tree allowed it to grow another top in a few years. Alta was still short on trees after the miners cut most of them for mining, so each one was precious.

Chic dragged the tree to the snowcat and then helped himself to a hot drink. He raised his cup wished everyone Merry Christmas and led the group in a few Christmas carols their—voices echoing through the cold mountain air. Falling snow covered the food on the table, and snowflakes hissed each time they hit the fire.

As darkness descended on the party, Mt. Superior faded into the snowy twilight and the lodge's lights twinkled. After much merriment, songs and good cheer, the engines of the snowcats roared to life. Some people piled in the back of the machines and others grabbed ropes and were towed behind on their skis. The snow had let up, and a few stars had emerged. The night promised to be icy cold. No one noticed the falling temperatures as the cats pulled up to the lodge. Wet, tired but happy people stomped their ski boots to knock off snow as they entered the lodge. The aroma of wet wool and pine needles almost overwhelmed the smell of dinner.

The festivities continued as the next evening traditionally was set aside for Christmas tree decorating and all the guests were invited. Most of them however, stood around and drank eggnog and supervised Maxine, Chic and me as my family put on ornaments and tinsel. On Christmas Eve day, Maxine would take fresh baked sugar cookies from Bob's kitchen and supervise lodge children in decorating—with more icing on the kids than the cookies but loads of laughter.

Christmas night was a wonderful dinner of turkey and all the trimmings. After dinner, there was a piñata party for kids in the lobby followed by Santa's coming to the Sitzmark Lounge for all the kids big and little. Of course Santa arrived by snowcat, not sleigh. Much later, when we were living at the house full-time, we had a Christmas party at which Santa also arrived by snowcat. Chic was driving the cat, and Santa was sitting in the back waving to everyone when Chic made an abrupt turn and off Santa flew into the snow. He was a good sport about it and didn't leave coal in Chic's stocking. The best part was, while Santa flew out, his sack with all the gifts stayed in the cat.

The lodge was full of families, many of whom came back year after year and knew each other. It was like having a huge extended family every Christmas and, for the tiny Morton family, this was a real treat.

When the holidays were over and guests had returned home, there was a new batch of skiers who braved the cold of January to ski.

Chic and Maxine decorating the Christmas tree at the Alta Lodge, circa 1960s

The duties of being a lodge owner were not all glamorous and fun. Dealing with sewage at Alta was always a challenge. Today sewer lines take the waste down into the valley, where it is treated accordingly. I do not have any exact data on this but, using my childhood memory, I would say that my father spent a great deal of his time unclogging toilets. In our house up on the hill, we had a marine toilet that used a fraction of the water that most toilets used at the time. This was important because each home and business had a holding tank that often needed to be pumped out sometimes before the winter was over and the summer road was plowed.

Our house was inaccessible by road for at least six months every winter, so we had to be careful not to fill up the tank. Alta Lodge and Snowpine Lodge both had open pit toilets in their basements. I was terrified as a child that I would fall in or drop something of value, like one of my dolls in there. I am sure that, when Chic signed on as manager of the lodge, he never envisioned himself becoming so intimate with plumbing or sewage.

I remember being taken to school by Edwin Gibbs, general manager of the Peruvian Lodge in a "honey wagon". I was mortified. But I am sure that he thought he was extremely clever getting rid of the sewage and getting the kids to school at the same time.

I also remember several Christmas Eves when Chic was dealing with toilets that were misbehaving rather than celebrating with his family.

Chic and Jean

CHAPTER #12

FISHING

Chic loved to ski; he loved Alta, Maxine and me; but he was passionate about fishing. I want to be very specific about the kind of fishing he loved—fly-fishing. In fact, often I was reminded that there was really no other form of real fishing. As a child, I remember him trying his luck in Little Cottonwood Creek where it slowed and meandered through Alta Valley. A few small fish were able to survive in that stream, and it only whetted his appetite for more.

For many years Chic, got his fix for fly-fishing in Wyoming in the Jackson Hole area. We had friends who owned and ran a dude ranch called the R lazy S and, while we were riding horses, he was fooling the wily fish and "wetting his flies" in those pristine waters. Later he went to Wyoming to see Jay Laughlin, one of the major stockholders in Alta Ski Lifts, and fish on his private land. This large and impressive ranch belonged to his wife's family.

In the early 1970s, Chic and his second wife, Jean, bought land south of Jackson in Star Valley and built a log fishing cabin. In fact, the cabin was built by Stu Thompson, who had patrolled at Alta for years before he started his log home building business. Chic and Jean both loved it there, and the fishing was outrageous in those early years. Star Valley is a ranching valley and, when times got lean, the ranchers would fish out those pretty little streams to stock their freezers; so when it was good, it was great.

After breakfast on a fishing day, Chic would sit on the screened-in porch and get his rod and flies ready for the day. Then he and Jean and whoever was visiting would load up in the truck and drive to the day's destination. Big streams and little creeks–it didn't matter as long as they had fish in them. Lunch was always packed in a cooler with lemonade and soft drinks. Jean never took to fishing, so she brought her book and ran a shuttle with the truck if it was needed.

The Mortons loved company at their cabin, and many people joined them for a weekend of fishing. It wasn't unusual to have not only all the beds filled but tents and trailers in the yard. Many of these people were Alta people who either worked or skied there.

I learned to fish to be a part of this scene. I got tired of being left at the truck and then not being part of the evening tales. Fly-fishing is not a sport for impatient people. It takes skill, which can be learned. But what it really is about is absolute concentration. When the rod bends and sends the line with the tiny fly over head to drop gently in the water, the excitement and focus is intense. That miniscule fly is sitting on top of moving water and eyes must be fixed on it until the fish lurking in the water rises and takes a sample of it. The adrenaline soars as the rod comes up and sets the hook, or pulls the fly out of the fish's mouth, or in my case, sometimes actually pulls the fish all the way out of the water and onto the bank.

Some of my fondest memories with Chic were wading with our hip boots, fighting through thick willows to access a clear little creek. We would leapfrog our way up the stream so that no one else fished the same stretch of water. Often I would just stand and watch as he cast his fly into a deep little hole and waited. When he would get a strike or land a fish, he would laugh from deep in his belly. Sometimes he would lead me to a favorite hole and tell me right where to place my fly to catch the big one. He was as thrilled with my catching a fish as if he had landed it himself.

One of his favorite fishing companions was my cousin Lynne, whom we called, Pooh, and was his brother, Jean's, oldest daughter. Lynne lived in Salt Lake City and was able to spend many weekends fishing with Chic. Lynne was an excellent fly fisherman and as passionate about the sport as Chic was. I was not there when the following incident happened but, as it has been told so many times, I feel as if I was with them that day. Wyoming is full of moose, big moose. Moose are unpredictable creatures that, on seeing a fisherman in their willows, may just keep eating, slowly walk away or charge. So it was always a good idea to be wary marching through the willows. During a past summer, Cousin Pooh had a harrowing experience with a moose while she was working in Jackson. If the doors of a nearby car had not been unlocked she would have been trampled by an irate female moose whose calf had been caught in a fence. Pooh had a great fear and respect for those creatures. She and Chic were fishing together one day and she was ahead of him. He had finished fishing and was walking back to the truck when he saw Lynne up river from him, frantically waving her arms and pointing. Chic couldn't see what she was pointing at and just went on to the truck. Well, she didn't come and she didn't come. Finally he drove up to where he had last seen her. There she was on the far side of the creek and on Chic's side was a large moose. The moose was ignoring her but he was in such a place she couldn't get to the road without disturbing him, which she wasn't about to do. Chic laughed and laughed at her when the moose finally left and she got back to the truck.

In the summer, Chic would work Monday through Thursday for the lift company and then he and Jean would drive up to Wyoming for a weekend of fishing. His dream was to retire and spend more time up there. Often they would stay a week at a time and use up some of his vacation. The evenings were spent telling fish stories and playing cards and other games. After he retired, he did spend most of the summers at the fishing cabin but a hip replacement at the age 70 left him too unsteady on his feet to fly-fish in the manner which brought him the most joy—which was wading in the streams. When doctors replaced his hip, they elongated his femur to try and match the other leg. But 50 years of a shortened leg had changed his entire body structure and, when he was "normal" again, he had difficulty walking. He gave up skiing and fly-fishing. It broke my heart and I missed his fishing laugh.

Chic even had fished in Alaska for BIG fish. He was flown into a lodge in the interior of Alaska where they fished for a week. I know that they had to beef up their lines, leaders and flies for the big ones. They cautioned the men to be aware of grizzly bears and not to surprise one. Chic, always a singer, sang and sang as he fished, hoping to let the bears know his location. I would have loved to watch him casting and singing "Little Joe the Wrangler" as his flies whizzed through the air and landed on the glassy, pristine water.

Springtime at Alta always came late. It loved to snow in April and May after the ski area was closed. It was a gloomy and depressing time. Chic would load Maxine and me in the car and drive to Mexico. We loved Mazatlan. Chic and Maxine had friends there who owned a hotel in downtown—Pat and Brownie, whose last names have gotten lost in my fading memories. We always rented an apartment out of town on the beach. In the month that we were there, Dad would fish in the surf as much as he could. It was an art to cast the line and keep from getting tumbled by the waves. He would be out for hours, jumping each time a wave came. Several times a day he would misjudge the size of a wave and it would slam him down. He always came up sputtering and laughing. It was a delightful way to spend the snowy spring after a busy winter by being away from Alta.

Chic's uneven legs often caused him to fall. He was as tough as nails, but his rod took the brunt as well as his body. He'd often come home wet with his rod broken. One summer when I was visiting in Wyoming, we walked into the upper Salt River to fish. It was about a three-mile-trek and part of the trail was high above the creek. Dad caught his bad leg on something and in a nano-second he was tumbling down the hill. My heart skipped a beat, but he was up brushing himself off and we continued on and fished all day. He was in his 60s when that happened and came home with a jammed thumb.

Earlier in Chic's life, before he was married to Maxine, he used to take horses into the Wind River Mountains in Wyoming to camp and fish. The Wasatch Mountain Club, to which Chic belonged, often took trips there to climb mountains. Chic went to fish. He told me that he once went by himself for a week to fish. He said he missed having someone to tell the tales of the daily fishing. Chic was a social man. Later, after he and my mother were married, he took her on a trip there to show her the spectacular country. I imagine them having an enjoyable time—just the two of them fishing and riding horses. On their way home from that trip, they stayed at a small log motel, which is still there, to rest and clean up before driving home. I was conceived in that motel.

I have explored the Wind River Mountains three different times and one of those times I carried my fly rod and took my turn at outwitting the wily mountain fish. It is rugged country with rough and craggy peaks rising out of valleys dotted with lakes and clear creeks taking mountain snowmelt to the lower agricultural valleys. The rock is granite, a severe rock of multiple colors that sparkles in the sun from flecks of quartz and mica. Each time I clambered around those mountains, I felt Chic there with me.

Chic ready to fish

CHAPTER #13

DOGS

S oft, silky ears, a wet nose and a welcoming lick from a favorite dog had always been a part of Chic's life. I know that several dogs graced his life before he was married. One of these dogs was named Butch, who was part German shepherd and part pit bull. Chic told the story about how this dog would carry a paper bag with eggs in it back from the store for Grace, Chic's mother, without breaking an egg. Chic never could believe the bad press that pit bulls received because Butch never ever showed aggression toward another dog or a person.

Our first family dogs were basset hounds. What amazing and docile creatures they were with their soft, floppy ears and sad eyes that never failed to solicit an exquisite ear rub from a guest of the lodge or one from his family. Maxine named our first basset Toulouse-Lautrec, after a famous French painter. Mr. Lautrec was afflicted with a genetic disorder that affected his growth. As an adult his torso was full grown but his legs were the same size as a child's. He was five feet tall and his legs were slightly longer than 27 inches. Basset hounds have a similar stature. Maxine had spent some time in Paris and was acquainted with the painter's work and obviously some of his history. It is also interesting that the painter had the same birth date as Chic, November 24. Toulouse was a dog of many attributes, one of these being his deep baying

Toulouse, the basset with a message

voice when he chased snowshoe rabbits through the willows with me trailing along adoringly behind him. A drawing of Toulouse was on the front of my birth announcements attesting to the fact that he was a true member of our family. He died when he fell into an open septic tank. It was such a sad day for a truly good friend.

Our second basset was named Casey Jones. Casey ran Alta Lodge. Chic and Maxine were just there to help, or so thought Casey. He was never an ordinary dog. He felt water dishes were beneath him. He drank his water from the water fountain in the lobby of the lodge. The fountain ran all the time and, though Casey often soaked his ears in the process, he was able to satisfy his thirst by putting his large paws on the fountain and drinking his fill. Chic always cringed, though the guests loved it he worried about the health department inspector seeing Casey's habit and, being appalled, putting a halt to the drinking fountain.

Casey and I spent many hours playing together in the snow. He loved to chase me down the hill in front of the Alta Lodge, either on my skis or in a sled. I had it easy–I would grab the ropetow and it would bring me back up the hill. Casey tried running back but, with his short little legs, he tired of that very quickly and resorted to grabbing the rope in his mouth and flopping over on his side to ride up. I would imagine that he burned his mouth a few time before he was successful. We lost Casey the day he fell in the Peruvian Lodge swimming pool when no one was around and he couldn't get out. It was a loss for us all.

We weren't finished with bassets the last one's name was Happy and happy he was with everyone. He would attach himself to whomever was hiking by, and eventually Chic gave him away to one of his admirers. He had tired of driving to collect him in Salt Lake or Park City.

One day Chic told Mom and me that he had seen an ad in the paper for Samoyed puppies and he was thinking of getting one. We had no idea what a Samoyed was other than they were used as sled dogs and had long white fur they sounded perfect for snow country. Our new dog's name was Sam he was a gorgeous dog with a large head and thick white fur. He was stubborn and independent but we loved him dearly. He and I shared many an adventure hiking and skiing together. We still lived at the lodge when Sam was young, and he preferred to sleep out in the snow. The guests were delighted when they would look onto the deck, see the snow move and out would emerge Sam. Sam loved to ski with me and chase the tips of my skis as they moved through the powder. He often chased me up the lift and then skied down barking. When the Albion Lift was built, we actually got him to ride with me up the chair. Chic was very fond of Sam. I know that he admired his independence and his desire for freedom. As Sam got older, we no longer could let him roam free and he wasn't as happy of a dog.

After we left the lodge, one of the employees got a Saint Bernard and named him Shaffer. Shaffer and Sam hated each other. Sam still felt that the Alta Lodge was his territory and

Shaffer knew it was his. A terrible war ensued between the two of them that was terrifying. I watched Shaffer try to jump through one of the picture windows at the lodge to get at Sam. Another time, I was driving past the lodge with Sam in the passengers seat when Shaffer came bounding out of the lodge after us. Sam went nuts and I watched him sink his teeth into the dashboard of our Ford Bronco. Shaffer was running alongside the car on the driver's side and Sam, foaming and biting, was determined to get to him. So, in a matter of seconds, Sam and I changed places. The car was still moving but he was now in the driver's seat. Shaffer jumped up and grabbed Sam by the neck and blood spattered all over the car. I was able to get my foot on the brake and dislodge them; and then I stepped on the gas and off we went, with Shaffer chasing after us and Sam growling and snarling out the back window.

Another incident happened when Chic used to take Sam to work with him to the lift building offices. If Shaffer was out, he would bound down the hill and chase the snowcat. Chic had enough of that, so he filled a squirt bottle with ammonia and sprayed it on Shaffer that didn't work he used a salt pellet gun. Shaffer wasn't the sharpest dog and he never learned to back away from the snowcat so the war also involved Chic and the cat.

This war continued into the summer, Chic and Sam had hiked down to the office. Shaffer was out walking with several of the lodge employees when he and Sam got into an altercation. Shaffer had him by the neck and was literally killing him. Chic picked up a pipe and told the people who were standing by watching and not doing anything that he was going to start at Shaffer's tail and work his way up his back, and if he didn't let go when he got to his head, he would kill him. Chic was mad. The employees took the pipe from Dad, and in desperation, he pushed the two dogs into the creek to break them up and went in himself. Dad came home covered in Sam's blood, dog saliva and soaking wet. Sam survived that one and so did Shaffer. The feuds continued for years and Sam had several scars on his face and a turned-in paw that left him with a limp to remind him of Shaffer. Ironically, Shaffer died of a heart attack when he jumped a small white dog and luckily the dog was unharmed. We were all dog lovers but none of us mourned that dog's passing.

When Jean came into our life, she had a little mutt named Lulu. Chic and I overcame our prejudice about smaller dogs and fell in love with her. She looked like a cross between a cocker spaniel and a small collie. She and Sam were my hiking buddies during high school, and I often took care of the dogs when Chic and Jean traveled.

After Sam died and Jean had to put Lulu down, they were convinced that they didn't want another dog—until Hobo. Dottie Weaver rescued Hobo and brought him to meet Chic and Jean at the house on Floribunda Drive in Salt Lake City. I wasn't there but I heard that it took Chic several seconds to attach himself to Hobo and vice versa. Hobo was a mix between a small poodle and Shiatsu—not at all a mountain dog. Hobo loved riding in the snowcat and Jean would put him in a small coat that she made especially for him. When they got home, Hobo would jump on Chic's lap and they both would take a nap. Later when Chic was recovering from his hip surgery, Hobo napped in his lap most of the day or at least when he wasn't begging for snacks. Jean put Hobo down when a back injury from falling through some steps became so severe and so painful that he was no longer able to move freely and it was his time to go.

Dogs were always a part of our life and, though the health department frowns on them in Alta, there are Alta Ski Lift avalanche dogs and a few pets that still roam the valley. I remember someone telling me that you can always tell a lot about the character of a person by how they treat their dogs. Chic treated our dogs like they were family—with kindness and attention as well as food, water and shelter. He would tell me that our dogs' needs came before ours because they depended on us for everything.

Sam

CHAPTER 14

CHIC'S ALTA

Alta means something different to each person who has experienced it. To some it is an exceptional ski area with amazing snow and challenging runs. Others realize the incredible beauty of the mountains and enjoy being immersed in that exquisite environment. For many it is a fun place to work and still others see it as a magical or spiritual place for solace.

Chic's Alta had many facets. It was the natural beauty of the peaks surrounding the Alta Valley that he loved. He lived in that environment through all the seasons and watched the peaks change their wardrobe in each one. He always felt a deep connection with the place; Chic commented in one of many interviews, "Alta was the best thing that ever happened to me." He cherished some and disliked others of the many different people who came through Alta during the 57 years he was involved in the canyon. It was his home, the place he met his wife, Maxine and his second wife, Jean. He raised his daughter, Kim in Alta. Alta was his extended family as much as Kim and Maxine and Jean were his immediate family. Chic built a home in Alta. It was not just of mortar and sticks, of glass and rocks, but a true home where people were welcomed with hospitality and comfort whether they were guests, employees or family.

It was his life's work running the lodge and the lift company. He was a gracious host and was able to juggle many different aspects of the two businesses. Alta Ski Lifts created many challenges for him but he was as proud of that company and its employees, lifts, cats, ski runs as if they were his own flesh and blood. He lived the credo that "ALTA IS FOR SKIERS".

"Alta is for Skiers", meant to Chic that the people, who came to Alta came for the snow and for the skiing. They were the purebloods of skiing. Chic's Alta was all about having the best quality skiing experience If that meant that they slowed the lifts down when much of the mountain was closed so that each skier had a great uncrowded run down, then that is what they did. He felt that it was better to stand in line than to have it crowded on the hill.

He wanted Alta Ski Lifts to do what it did best and that was manage skiing, so the lift company was not directly involved in food service, rentals or retail. Alta Ski Lifts managed the mountain and the lifts, grooming, ski school and ticket sales. They owned both the Watson's Shelter and the Alpenglow buildings but leased out the food service operations. Chic believed in locals being able to ski, so during his reign lift tickets were the least expensive in the industry. He wanted to see local families being able to ski as much as possible. Chic's statement to a local magazine says it all; "It's been our philosophy all along that we keep the capacity of our lifts low at what we think the runs will take to give people a good ski."

In an interview for a major newspaper, a New York skier was asked what was different about Alta and he said, "Alta has soul." Chic's comment on hearing that was, "There's feeling in Alta, all Alta, and most of the people are very emotional about it. Some people are financially able to ski anywhere in the world but they just become, like the rest of us, addicted to Alta. It becomes a personal place to them."

Chic, directed by his board of directors, was able to keep Alta's lift ticket prices low. In 1990, it cost $19 a day to ski when other ski areas were charging $40 or above. Chic stated in an interview when he was asked how they kept the cost of tickets so low.

"We don't go into equity debt, so we haven't big interest charges hanging over us we pass some of that savings on to the customer."

In a November 1981 issue of Ski Area Management, an industry periodical, in an article on Alta, "The Alta Enigma," explained that some of Alta's Camelot-like procedures would send shivers through most resort board rooms because it's based on selling the best product at the most reasonable cost."

> "Alta, the quaint Utah ski resort with world class stature, is perplexity personified. When ski lift tickets at comparable resorts cost $20, Alta apologetically charges $10. When other resorts install triple and quadruple chairlifts to get more skiers on the mountains sooner, Alta runs its lifts below capacity. When other resorts shell out megabucks for expensive advertising budgets, Alta has no such budget. When skyrocketing interest rates are a nemesis of other resorts, Alta enjoys a healthy return from high-yield certificates of deposit."

Chic believed in a simple philosophy of business, sell the best product at the most reasonable cost. Chic felt that the competition of other ski areas was not an issue. He commented that Alta had not changed its operating policies due to competition. He believed that if you treated the guests right you didn't need to worry about the other ski areas. One of his favorite sayings was, "Frankly, we get more customers from them than they get from us. Many people don't like the bigness and we have the best–or some of the best–snow and ski conditions that you will find anywhere." Chic felt that the customers of Alta would do the advertising for them by having a quality ski experience. This way Alta could put that advertising money back into the mountain.

Chic wanted everyone who skied at Alta to get as inexpensive a lift ticket as Alta could manage. Because of this, Alta did not offer group discounts, discount coupon programs or cheaper children's tickets. When a large group would approach Chic for a discount, they were appalled when Chic would reply that, if they could find comparable ski conditions at prices lower than Alta's, they should go there and most of them came to Alta.

Much of Alta's success, other than Mother Nature's abundant snowfall, was due to the longevity of key employees, including minimum personnel turnover among supervisory staff. During Chic's time as resort manager, he had some 30 supervisors on the payroll year-round. Historical characters like Buck Sasaki had been in charge of the operation and maintenance of lifts since 1942, with Hans Brogle at his side since1953, then Alf Engen from the beginning. All helped in the operation of the lift company. Of course, the two major stock holders, Joe Quinney and Jay Laughlin, all contributed to the consistency of policy and product for Alta.

Chic's Alta was a patchwork with many people and plenty of interesting experiences. Listening to their stories gives a more complete picture of Chic at Alta.

Chic in front of a partially finished Alta house

"DOC" AND DOTTIE WEAVER

In 1964, when Rob and Dottie Weaver bought Max Lumberg's house below the Peruvian Lodge, they were already in love with Alta and wanted to spend more time there. After a few years, they bought a lot on the east side of Albion Basin and built an A- frame cabin. It was November, and they were still in the process of building when snowstorms shut down the road to the house and the ski area opened. They still had some material they wanted to get to the building site. Dottie thought about Chic Morton at Alta Ski Lifts and wondered if they would loan one of their snowcats. So, even though Dottie didn't know Chic very well, she marched into his office and asked if she and Rob could use some of the Alta Ski Lifts snowcats to take their stuff to the cabin. At that time, they only had a snowmobile with a trailer. Chic's reply was, "Absolutely not," using his most stern Chic expression. After a moment's pause, he continued, "But what I will do for you is, if you have all of your supplies at the bottom of the Albion Chair before the lift opens, we can haul your stuff up and you can use your snowmobile to get it from there." True to his word, everything worked out and they got their supplies to the house. This was the start of a long and wonderful friendship between the Weavers and the Mortons.

Many of us were victims of Chic's gruff exterior and demeanor, and we learned very quickly that was he was more growl than bite.

I was curious what it was like in Alta during the time the Weavers lived there so I asked Dottie and she commented that she thought that the 1960s and 1970s were the most romantic years at Alta. She felt that most of the people there, whether living or working, were there for the same reasons and got along well and mostly enjoyed each others company. In fact, she is still friends with most of those folks and still keeps in touch.

Rob and Dottie were proud of their new little house and wanted to show it off to Chic so in the late 1960s, when their A-frame was livable, they invited Chic up for dinner one night. Chic's response was uncharacteristically soft; he answered their query with, "I have a guest." Dottie answered, "Well, bring him along." Chic, with a big grin, replied, "He is a her." It turned out that the "her" was Jean, and it was one of their first dates.

Not only were Jean and Chic and Rob and Dottie friends, their dogs were in love with each other. The Weavers had a big female black lab named Silky. She was a gorgeous dog, or that is what Chic's Samoyed, Sam, thought. Sam always knew when Silky was at the Weaver's cabin and he would trot the mile up to the basin to pick her up and off they would meander to the campground to dump over the trash cans. Rob would notice Silky was missing and he would comment, "I'm sure Sam is up here. I'll go get them and call Chic and Jean."

During the winter, Sam would curl up outside their door in the snow and wait for Silky. Once he startled a guest who opened the door just as Sam pushed his head up out of the snow, where he had been buried during his wait, and shook like a polar bear.

Rob was one of Chic's best friends, and their friendship would last until they both died in 1997. Dottie reflected that she thought Rob and Chic were such good friends because they shared similar political views and were both "curmudgeons".

When I was interviewing Dottie, she made the comment that she felt that Chic knew the mountains at Alta like the back of his hand. He and Jean had been at Rob and Dottie's house for dinner one night in another of Alta's famous snowstorms. It was snowing several inches an hour, the wind was blowing snow so hard it was making visibility impossible and they got lost on the way home. To make matters worse, it was dark when they left the Weaver's house and got into their snowcat. Chic called later when they had reached the house safely and said that, at one point, they had totally lost their way and found that he and Jean were on the edge of Snake Pit, a deep ravine permanently closed to skiers due to extreme avalanche danger. They backed up and made it home, but it was a humbling experience.

In the summer of 2011, when Dottie took Rob's ashes up into Albion Basin to scatter, she stopped at the old Morton house site and spread some ashes there too. She said, "I knew those two would want to be together." Chic's ashes are buried on the land where the Morton house stood for almost 50 years.

Chic and Rob Weaver

JIM AND ELFREDA SHANE

Jim Shane was another figure in Chic's life at Alta. Chic had met both him and his wife, Elfreda, through the Wasatch Mountain Club, where they hiked and skied together. They took several trips together into the Wind River Mountains to fish and climb. Jim began his time at

Alta on the ski patrol while he also was going to school at the University of Utah to become an electrical engineer. Later, after Jim had practiced as an engineer, he and Elfreda built the Gold Miner's Daughter, which was the newest lodge at Alta. The original building only had 12 rooms, but they later expanded to more than 200 rooms. Jim and Elfreda were managing their lodge at the same time Chic and Maxine were at the Alta Lodge, but Elfreda said they didn't see much of each other because they were so busy at each of their own lodges working seven days a week all winter.

BINX SANDAHL

Binx was one of the snow rangers at Alta in the 1960s. A handsome man with a head of silver hair and a quick smile. His nickname was "The Silver Fox;" he was a fun- loving and handsome man.

He often had to be the one to tell Chic that they weren't going to open the road in time; and sometimes they didn't get it open until 1pm. Chic was understandably upset, and Binx relates the following story about his interaction with Chic.

"Chic used to get so damn mad at me and the Forest Service that I was afraid to go and see him. In fact, I worked out this system: I'd walk up to Chic's office door and throw my hat in. If Chic threw it out, I knew he was too mad to talk; if he didn't, I'd kind of slink into his office and test the waters. But you know, we really couldn't speed up the process. Chic felt it was the Forest Service's responsibility to provide avalanche forecasting and control because Alta was on National Forest; the Forest Service felt they could not afford to hire any more snow rangers just so Alta could open on time and make more money. So, it was a standoff. By the way, let me emphasize, that while Chic Morton was ornery as hell, I always knew where Chic was coming from. The man had a heart of gold and was always a pleasure to work with."

ONNO WEIRINGER

Onno came to Alta from Montana to patrol when he was 20 in 1972 and now sits behind the desk of the general manager of Alta Ski Lifts. Though recently the office was remodeled, Onno sat at the same desk that Chic had used for many years.

Onno didn't go looking for Chic's job. In fact, he was satisfied with his position as snow safety director, and he really liked his job. So, when Chic called him into his office and, from his famous chair where he slumped comfortably, his blue eyes looking directly at Onno, he said, "I want to talk to you about taking my job. I'm about ready to quit." Onno was surprised and responded by saying he really liked his job and didn't want to change. Chic's response was, "That's fine. How are you going to like working for someone else; 'cause if you don't want it, then I will get someone else you can work for them." Onno took a few moments to think about that proposal, and here he is today managing the lift company from the corner office at the Lift Hauf. He still looks out his office at the same view as Chic—the bottom terminals of the Collins and Wildcat chairs. Here he makes many of the same decisions that Chic did and is also challenged with new things. The ski business is different now and Alta has adjusted to many of those changes, including high speed detachable lifts, food service, environmental upgrades, planting trees and possible expansion into the Grizzly area. Skiers today are as interested in how many runs they can make as the quality of the powder snow. Onno believes that skiing back when Chic was in charge was a very different beast. It was a family of skiing and everyone did their part to make it work. Now it is a hard-core business with aggressive competition and more technology, though the basic premise of taking people up the mountain to go skiing is still the same. Chic ran Alta Ski Lifts as a business but it was much more relaxed than it is now with the corporate world taking over skiing. The stakes are bigger. The passion of skiing is no longer in the forefront of the business; it is all about making money.

Onno remembers a time when he worked as the snow safety director and got in big trouble with Chic. He chuckled softly as he began his story. Back in March 1981, there was a major avalanche cycle going on at Alta and big, wet slides had been running regularly. Onno had been monitoring the snowpack on High Rustler and was concerned about its stability. Not only was it a favorite run for locals but an easy way down cut across near the bottom of the run for less experienced skiers. This "cat track" also accessed other runs and would have plenty of skiers on it, possibly in harm's way.

Onno wanted to give it an explosive test to see if it would run before it went on its own. He went into Chic's office to talk to him about it. Chic didn't want anything to do with it; after all, it was close to the end of the ski season. "Let it wait," he said. But Onno wanted to do it anyway and Chic's comment was, "Go ahead, but nothing better go wrong." Onno felt confident and responded, "No problem."

They waited until the end of the day when everyone was off the mountain and set the charges. There were several seconds of delay before Onno watched in horror as the entire slope broke loose and in places clear down to the ground. The snow ran across the cat tracks and into the flats by the transfer tow and started up the hill toward the lodge. It took out some trees and, when it finally stopped, it was a jumble of huge chunks of snow mixed with pieces of trees. Onno was aghast and. as he was checking the debris at the bottom of the slide to make sure everyone was safe, he heard Chic's Imp snowcat rumble to life and he knew that he had only moments until Chic arrived at the slide scene. Onno directed Chic to a safe way around the debris and, as the cat drove by him on his way home, he looked in and saw Chic's "grump face" and then he lifted his arm to give him his infamous middle finger. Onno didn't sleep very well that night. Onno chuckled again recalling walking into Chic's office and said, "I had to throw my hat in when I went in the next day and I was afraid it would fly back out." Chic was mad, but Onno survived to work many more ski seasons.

It is important at this juncture to stop and explain about Chic's unusual manner of expressing his displeasure. He had an interesting way of displaying his middle finger; he carefully curled back his index and forth finger so that all the knuckles were lined up and then lifted that naughty middle finger straight up. In Onno's case, Chic was truly mad but, in other instances, he was literally telling someone that he or she had overextended their boundaries or was full of it.

Hoopa

Hoopa–Dave Robertson–who has been a ski school instructor for many years at Alta and is now the director of the Alf Engen Ski School, was called into Chic's office over some infraction that no one remembers. He was nervous when he sat down across from Chic, who proceeded to dress him down quite severely. Chic was sitting in his usual posture leaning back with his legs out in front of him. Hoopa left his office feeling pretty low about getting in trouble. So, on his way out he stopped by the office of Hans and Buck for some cheering up. They explained to Hoopa that you weren't really in trouble unless his hands were balled up tight on his thighs. If he was just mildly annoyed, he would be flipping you the bird with the other hand lying relaxed on his thigh.

Another Chic incident that involved Hoopa happened when he brought back a bunch of fireworks from New Hampshire. He thought it would be great to set them off on New Year's Eve. It was a great display and, when the last explosion went off with a big bang, it echoed off the mountains like a huge cannon. Hoopa again was called into Chic's office and he was a bit nervous about the outcome. Chic gave him a little grief about setting off the fireworks without permission and things were a bit tense for a few minutes. Then he grinned and admitted that it was a good idea to have fireworks displayed after the torchlight on New Year's Eve. It is still a tradition and Hoopa is still working at Alta.

KAREN AND BOB TRAVIS

Karen and her husband, Bob, worked at the Peruvian Lodge when they first came to Alta in 1967. She started off as a supervisor in charge of room and the cafeteria and Bob was the manager of the lodge. They then bought into the Snowpine lodge, but sold to their partner Allen Cap and went back to the Peruvian to manage ski and rental shop.

Karen remembers that Alta was more comfortable, looser and not as busy in those early days when everyone knew everyone else. Most employees lived on the mountain and in tight living conditions, whether it was at one of the lodges, for the lift company or one of the mountain restaurants. Because of these conditions, people became very close. They worked together, and there had to be plenty of cooperation.

After the Peruvian Lodge, Karen and Bob wanted a change so they took over the Watson Shelter and worked closely with Chic and Alta Ski Lifts. The shelter was named after "Mayor Watson," who was responsible for getting skiing at Alta started. Bob and Karen started the first elegant sit-down restaurant on the mountain, upstairs in the old Watson Shelter. Originally it had been only a shelter to get out of the cold, so this elegant restaurant with white linen table clothes, silverware and china, fuzzy slippers to replace cold ski boots and good food was a far cry from those early shelter days. Bob and Karen respected Chic and who he was and what he had done at Alta so they named that restaurant after him—Chic's Place. It operated until Bob and Karen retired from the business and decided also to retire the name. There is now a beautiful new Watson's and it has its own fine restaurant, which is called the Collin's Grill.

Bob always said of Chic that you may disagree with him but he was always fair. No matter what he tells you, even if it isn't what you want to hear, you know that he has put some thought into it. Bob thought Chic ran a one-man company.

Karen remembers the early Alta Chamber of Commerce, which was created to help promote the businesses at Alta. Each lodge owner was a member, and Chic represented Alta Ski Lift's interests. At their first meeting, they chose straws to see who would be mayor and Lee Bronson from the Rustler Lodge was the "winner." I know Chic let out a sigh of relief that he "lost."

Karen remembers that the chamber meetings were often "butting" heads to get things accomplished. She says it reminded her of the three Alta dogs during that time—Baron, a Great Dane from the Peruvian Lodge Shaffer, a St. Bernard from the Alta Lodge; and Sam, the Samoyed owned by Chic and whose place was at the lift company offices and the Alta House. These three dogs staked out their territories and would fight about it. It wasn't all that different with the businesses, lodge owners and lifts but somehow they came to some agreements and were able to get things accomplished. When Alta became a town, Chic sat on the town council. It was something he needed to do but it was also an aggravation to him as there was always so much infighting.

When the Travis's or any other employee or visitor came to Chic's office, he exuded a large presence in his small no-frills office. Karen remembers that, "He filled his office and that chair."

Chic seemed to know everything that was going on around Alta. He had good vision, good hearing and an excellent pair of binoculars. His office sat in the corner of the lift building with a porch running around the outside and into the bunk house. It housed the single men who worked for the company, and no women were allowed in the dorms. However, in the mornings as Chic sat at his desk, he would watch a small parade of women leaving the buckhorn. It was affectionately called, "The Parade of Shame." Chic used this information mostly for teasing and seemed amused by the morning parade. He also watched from our house on the hill above Alta to see who was visiting whom and at what lodge. I never heard him use this information in a vicious manner, only for fun. He also kept in touch with the happenings at Alta with a radio that monitored the ski patrol, cat crew, ski school and road crew; he had one in his office and at the house. There wasn't much that got by him. I have heard that the employees had their own radio code if something needed to get by Chic. Chic would say about Alta, "It is a very, very small town."

Bob remembers when they would go to Watsons in the morning to work they knew if they saw a set of tracks walking up, it was their employee and if they were crooked they knew he had a tough night and so it would be a challenging day for them all.

I often went with Dad on his rounds on the mountain. He always stood in line and, though he didn't take notes, he was watching the lifts, the way the lines moved, what the employees were doing, listening to conversations around him. We didn't get much skiing in, but I found it interesting to see the mountain through his eyes. Ski area management is a multi–faceted and often complicated business. The business needs to make its total yearly income in a little over five months and most of that revenue comes in two weeks at Christmas, holiday weekends and spring break. Training and hiring employees happens every year and having returning employees is a bonus. Chic had many loyal employees year after year. The reason they stayed is that they loved Alta and Chic was good to them. It was imperative to keep a thumb on everything going on, always.

In the 1960s and 1970s it was for the love of skiing and the mountains that kept employees coming back year after year. When Karen first started at the Peruvian Lodge, she was making $50 per month, plus room and board, and she still had to pay for her own $5 lift ticket. The popular thing to do back then was buy a 10-punch ticket and hope it didn't get punched every time you skied. Alta also sold single ride tickets back then, and Eilfreda Shane recounts that one of the lift operators would collect the single ride ticket but not destroy them and then that night at the bar he would trade tickets for beers. I'm sure if Chic had found out that would've ended immediately as well as the person's job at Alta Ski Lifts.

While Chic was managing Alta Ski Lifts, free or discounted lift tickets were a rare thing. He really did believe in giving everyone a discount with less expensive tickets than most areas. Only other ski area owners and managers got free tickets. I recall that my stepmother, Jean, was working, at the main ticket office when a very handsome and rugged man asked for an Alta Star Pass, which was a free pass at Alta back then. She said "no" and then he went on to explain that his name was Robert Redford. Jean had no idea who that was and still said "no". The other women in the office were giggling behind her and she wasn't quite sure what was going on. Mr. Redford explained patiently to her that he was the owner of a ski area named Sundance. So, she called Chic on the phone and asked him what the deal was with the Redford guy. Chic laughed heartily and said to go ahead and give him one. He teased her about that for years. I often wonder if Robert Redford found it a bit refreshing not to be recognized. He often skied at Alta and kept a low profile.

When I was growing up at Alta, I always had either a ten punch pass or later on a season pass. When I came back to visit after I was married, my husband and I went into Dad's office to find out about a ticket. He strongly stated that now that I was married I was no longer his daughter and wouldn't get a free pass. He and I had a few words about that and he ended up buying us our passes while we were there. He felt strongly about not giving away free tickets, that was for sure.

LAUREL MCKENNY

Laurel came to Alta as a young 19 year old and she describes herself as quiet and shy. So, when Merlyn Berg gave her the nickname of "Lusty" she decided it was contrast to her personality. The person I know as Lusty had a great laugh and a 'lust' for life that was contagious, so I would have to say that her name was appropriate.

Lusty reflects that Chic was known for his dry humor as she explains in the following story. It was during a monstrous snowstorm that Lusty, a long time Alta employee, learned about Chic's propensity for teasing. Lusty was working the front desk at the Gold Miner's Daughter when someone came in saying that a car had been hit in the parking lot. Lusty ran out to investigate still in her dress clothes and shoes, traipsing through the snow and, sure enough, her car was smashed. It had been hidden under the many feet of snow that had fallen in the past days and had been hit by the Alta Ski Lifts snowplow. The very next day, Lusty was called into Chic's office to talk about it. She felt a bit apprehensive going in it as if she was talking to her father when she nervously took a chair across from Chic and he said to her, "Now Lusty, you have been working here long enough to know that you should have at least marked your car." He was smiling at her and his eyes were twinkling so she relaxed a bit. Alta Ski Lifts did pay for her car, and she never left it unmarked again.

Lusty's first season at Alta was 1964-65. She and some friends had gone up to Logan to talk to a guy who worked at Alta to get the scoop on how to get a job there. He gave them two names–Edwin Gibbs, who was the owner of the Peruvian Lodge, and Chic Morton. Lusty started working at Alta in the Peruvian Lodge. Lusty was always one of Chic's favorite girls working at Alta. He appreciated her sense of humor and her willingness to tease him back.

Alf, Evelyn and Chic in front of the Alta Lodge

THE ENGEN FAMILY

Chic's life was interwoven with many people, including Alf Engen and his family. Alf and Chic were not only friends but worked closely together as Alf was the director of the Alta Ski School for many years. In the summer Chic, Maxine, Alf and his wife, Evelyn, would travel together to Mexico, Canada and Minnesota, fishing. Alf and Evelyn had two boys, Alan and Johnny. Alan followed in his father's footsteps in the ski business and ski jumping, after a successful career at Hercules Company, he became the school director and then director of skiing at Alta.

Alan tells the story about the time Chic and one of his female friends were riding one afternoon and stopped by the house Alf was building for his family in Salt Lake City on 62nd South. Young Alan was fascinated with Chic's horse and wondered if he could ride it. Chic lifted him up, but the horse had other ideas and took off with Alan clutching the saddle with all his strength. Chic jumped on his friend's horse, galloped after the runaway and brought him back safe and sound, if not a little dazed.

Alf and Evelyn had a room in the basement of the Alta Lodge which was next to the Morton's rooms. Over his young life, Alan would spend many days at the lodge and actually missed plenty of school in the process. One particular March night in 1952 would stand out in the minds of those two families for many years. Around 3 am, two avalanche slide paths above Alta Lodge let loose at the same time. The avalanche split right above the upper guard station; one section flew toward the Peruvian Lodge and the other smashed into the west side of the Alta Lodge. It went through the dining room and hit the fireplace in the lobby. Of course, under the lobby were the Morton and Engen families, fast asleep. The snow came into the window of Alf's room and buried him and Evelyn up to their waists but it buried Alan completely. Alf quickly dug Alan out, and Chic came running into their room. When he saw the devastation he said, "Jesus Christ." Once he and Alf were sure that Evelyn and Alan were safe and comfortable in Chic's apartment, he and Alf went off to see if anything was left of the lodge and if anyone was hurt. Though no one was hurt, Chic and Alf had a long, long night ahead of them. It was one of two times that the lodge was actually hit by an avalanche during Chic's years at Alta.

Alan's experience with Chic at Alta was a positive one; he felt that Chic was an important cog in the development of Alta. He felt that no matter what the situation was you always knew where you stood with Chic. He was blunt, he said it just the way it was. Not many things happened at Alta in which Chic wasn't involved. As in other ski areas, there were always people who were trying to ski for free. Some people tried to forge tickets; they most often were caught, and Chic was always involved. He was harsh but equitable.

An example of his unusual bluntness is around the way he dealt with unhappy customers. Typically they would come into his office to complain about something they didn't feel was right, which ranged from the condition of the snow, the weather, or how they had been treated. He would listen and listen to them and, if he felt they were justified, he would take care of them. However, if he felt that they were wrong or whining, he would ask to see their pass if they were a season passholder, he would say, "I'm afraid, sir, that we can't make you happy we will be sending you a pro-rated refund on your pass and we would appreciate your not coming back." He shocked many a passholder. He was not afraid to tell them that they might like the ski area down the road, Snowbird, better. He truly believed that what Alta had was unique and wonderful and, if people weren't happy, they didn't need to ski there. Often, management is so afraid of losing customers they will give into their demands, no matter the circumstance. Chic was not like that.

Sometimes, when people work a long time together their lives become entwined together like the paintbrush, a colorful mountain flower that entwines its roots with other plants to survive. So it wasn't a surprise when Alf and Chic died within days of each other in the same nursing home. I went to see Alf just after Dad died. He was very distraught and said, "I just don't know if I can live after my dear friend has gone." He didn't, and the ski world lost two giants of skiing.

RUSS HARMER

Among one of the many employees who worked for Chic over the years was Russ Harmer. He was one of those young people who came to find a job for a few years and stayed for most of his life. Alta is more than a ski area; it is a way of life for Russ and many other skiers.

Russ was the head of the "cat crew." He managed the maintenance shop that kept not only the snowcats running but the other ski lift equipment as well. For instance, he also kept up the company trucks. Russ conveyed to me that Chic flew around the rough roads of Alta like a "bat out of hell." Russ was never sure what the hurry was, but Chic obviously had his reasons for beating up his truck. I find that interesting because he always seemed to know when I drove the Bronco too fast on the washboard roads and would get after me to slow down.

Russ started working at Alta in December 1966. That next summer, he helped put in the Sugar Loaf Lift, which expanded into the Albion Basin Area which was previously backcountry skiing only. Russ remembers that Buck Sasaki was in charge of that expansion. Back then, lift manufacturers didn't install lifts like they do now so it was up to the summer crew. Russ hauled all the materials for the lifts and the new roads. He had found an all-wheel-drive truck that had its cab cut off so that they could haul the lift towers up steep roads. He had many wild rides up and down those roads that summer. Five of the towers were put in by helicopter, which was an adventure in itself. This was the first time they had done that at Alta.

For several summers before the lift was put in, Chic and Buck had been walking that mountain deciding where the towers should go and where the bottom and top terminal were to be located. It was an exciting time for Alta to be opening all new lift-accessed skiing. Russ helped decide where several of the runs would be–Roller Coaster and Devil's Elbow.

Russ remembers Chic as stern but fair. An example of this was the time he and Red Altum had decided to sneak off on a little trip during the middle of the winter. Heck, there hadn't been any new snow and things in the cat house were under control and Red was in charge of snow removal. So, they hopped into Red's truck, drove to Sun Valley and then Jackson Hole. Alta is a small place, and sometimes employees just had to get away. On their way back, they called Alta and found out it was snowing like crazy so they broke all speed limits getting home.

They did get back in time to get all the plowing done; Chic's response was a stern look and a warning that this was as close as they had ever come to being fired. In other words, don't do it ever again.

Chic liked to have his thumb on the pulse of Alta all the time. Russ got on Chic's bad side one time after he went around Chic to Joe Quinney. It was all about getting a couple of snowmobiles to help the ski patrol move injured skiers from the back side of the mountain across the flats to the patrol room. Chic stubbornly refused after numerous requests. He just didn't like snowmobiles. Russ took the initiative to talk to Joe one day when he was up at the area and Joe thought it was a great idea. Since Joe was a major stockholder, what he said pretty much was how it was. Chic was pretty unhappy when Russ did that; he received a good dressing down and, when Russ was sufficiently contrite, Chic admitted that it was a good idea.

Russ felt that working at Alta was just like having a large, extended family. He felt that Chic treated his employees like they were part of the family and Jean loved having all of them up to house for parties. It wasn't often that Chic told anyone that they were doing a good job, but you knew immediately when you weren't. Looking back on my childhood, I would have to agree with Russ's assessment. I always knew when I had crossed the line, yet the sweetest words he ever said, were that he was proud of me.

Russ met his wife, Jeannie, at Alta. Their first home together was Rob and Dottie's cabin in Albion Basin, which they bought in 1973. Russ did quite a bit of work on the cabin, including bringing in winter water. Like Chic, they had to use a snowcat to get to and from their house.

They had several adventures coming and going to their house, including being hit by avalanches twice. The first time they were hit, the slide slammed into their snowcat and they literally flew through the air. When the slide stopped, they were buried. Russ was able to get a window open and dug a small pocket in the snow to get air. He always carried a radio and an avalanche beacon. His crew got his plea for rescue so they hurried to locate and dig him and Jeannie out. Later that same winter, they were hit again below Greeley Bowl. It seems that there was a miscommunication between the ski patrol and Russ. The night after being hit by the second slide, Jeannie and Russ stayed at Chic and Jean's house. The next year they moved to town. Before they left, a slide hit the back of their cabin and Jeannie was done with so much adventure in her daily life.

Avalanche

BILL BINGER

Another story of a young man coming to Alta to spend a winter patrolling and staying a lifetime is Bill Binger's. In 1972, after finishing his degree, Bill was on a grand tour of the West mostly to ski, when he met Court Richards, ski patrol director at Alta, while they were both in Grand Targee, Wyoming. Court told him to come to Alta and ski before he went back home, which he did, and not only fell in love with Alta but asked for a job with the patrol. Bill still has a hand-written letter offering him a job working six days a week, eight hours a day for $200 a month plus room and board. He couldn't have been happier. He worked two full seasons before he went back to school to become a dentist. He worked and went to school part-time to finish his prerequisites for dental school. He and another patrolman shared one job. Bill did control work in the morning, went to school and came back in the afternoon. Chic was supportive of Bill's going back to school. In fact, Chic was thrilled when Bill received a phone call from the school in California about his acceptance. Chic called Bill on the radio because he was patrolling at the time and was on top of Mt. Baldy. Chic said he might want to return this call from the university in southern California as soon as possible; they wanted to talk to him. Bill hightailed it down the Baldy Chutes at record speed to return the call. Dental school was a way for Bill to support his skiing habit and later his family. He had his practice in Salt Lake City and he still had Alta. He liked dentistry because it was a good combination between art and science. He had graduated with an undergraduate degree in economics and a minor in comedy and poetry. Bill has a poem or a song for every event or occasion.

The first time Chic and Jean had the patrol up to the house for a party, Bill and a few others put together a skit and songs to entertain everyone. It was a great hit. Even after Bill left, he always visited Chic when he came back from school. Later, Bill would be both Chic and Jean's dentist. Chic was always ready for a good laugh and some fun; he really got into the spirit of things when Bill put together the first annual Alta Prom, which was a patrol reunion. He dressed up in his black hat and string tie.

Another example of Bill's fun nature was the time he wanted to write a spoof on the Alta Powder News for April Fool's Day. When he approached Will Pickett, the editor, about it, he didn't think Chic would go for it. But Bill knew about Chic's sense of humor; when he told him his plan and showed him a sample paper, he said he would have to read it through. In the end, not only was he supportive of it but Alta Ski Lifts paid for printing.

Chic was really good to Bill and later his wife, Dianne. They had met at a party in the Buckhorn, where Bill saw this gorgeous woman and knew he was in love. After they were married and had kids, one afternoon Dianne called the main office of Alta Ski Lifts about a somewhat embarrassing situation; Chic immediately got on the radio and told Bill, "Mr. Bill, your wife has left a message for you; something about forgetting your child at daycare." I'm sure both Dianne and Bill got plenty of teasing for that incident, especially since it went out over the radio and his entire fellow patrolmen heard it.

Bill felt that talking to Chic wasn't much different than talking to his father, who was an engineer and always quizzed Bill about things. Chic always wanted to know all the details of any project that Bill wanted to do and Bill knew to come prepared. He felt that Chic could be pretty tough; he had earned every line on his face. He was a bit intimidating and not always approachable but he did project as a caring and gentle man. He cared that things were right on the mountain; he cared about the employees and he expected a lot of them. He also had a playful side to him. At Christmas, he would bring a bottle of Jack Daniels into the patrol room and stay as the patrol passed around for swigs. It was a few years later when the bottle was again passed and it came back half full. Chic commented that things were certainly changing around Alta as he grinned at the aging patrolmen. His sense of humor was a bit dry but very evident. He always got a chuckle out of Bill's pranks.

Bill remembers Alta of the 1960s and the 1970s as being unique; it was a time when people were able to make a living from skiing. It attracted a certain kind of person, and the relationships that were forged there lasted a lifetime. It was a time of BIG avalanches, helping people and lots of road and inter-lodge closures. There was an intimacy at Alta at that time, and if you were part of the ilk, you stayed; if not, you left. When Snowbird opened, a few went down the road but the ones who stayed were true Alta folks. Alta was about people, pleasure and great skiing. People who were there were committed to a unique experience.

When Chic retired, he was given a watercolor painting that portrayed the view from the porch of our Alta house looking down canyon toward Mr. Superior. The town of Alta is snuggled in the valley and the mountains reach upward toward an early evening sky. It is an exquisite painting. Bill was responsible for getting the painting commissioned and having prints made to pay for the it. Later, Alf was given one of Alfs High Rustler, too. As Bill said, "It was a risk but the cause behind it was so worth it–Chic."

Chic receiving his retirement painting.

BARBARA ALTUM

Behind every great man there are amazing women. Chic was no exception; Maxine, Emilie, Jean, and the women who sat at their desks outside his office and helped with phones, answering questions, doing secretarial work, accounts receivable, and other odds and ends. There were a few that passed through this position during Chic's tenure at Alta Ski Lifts. Some names that come to mind: Suzie Haskins, Sam Carey and Barb Altum. These gals didn't have the option of throwing in their hats to see what kind of mood he was in before they entered his office. They saw the best and the worst and they enjoyed working for him.

Barb Altum, who still works at Alta, said of Chic, "As a boss, he was wonderful." She went on to explain that she enjoyed his sense of humor, his patience, and his stories. Often, Chic would be puttering around his office or sitting at his desk singing. He had a great voice and would break into song when he felt like it. The lyrics to his songs often were very colorful. Suzie Haskins would blush when she listened to the words. Barb enjoyed hearing him sing. She knew that Chic scared some people but she was able to banter with him and also stood up to him when needed. When she first started with Chic she had no accounting experience and he was patient with her learning. He taught her good sound accounting techniques that she still uses and he recommended that she always double-check her figures.

Chic's schooling was in accounting and so he did all of the journal entries for the lift company plus he figured out the payroll with his secretaries' help. On Monday of every week of the ski season, all of the weekly ticket sales had to be balanced. This was all done without the help of computers. My cousin Connie Norpell, now Marshal, was the department head of the ticket office for many years and was accountable to Chic for those reports. She learned very early on that she could not walk over to his office without being very certain that she had been as clear and concise on the report as possible. It was always a bit nerve-racking for her.

When Chic no longer had his own horses to ride, he would take Maxine and me to the R Lazy S dude ranch in Jackson Wyoming. Not only did he get to ride horses, but it was also great fly fishing. He met Barb at the ranch, where she was working summers off from her schoolteaching job. She later married Red Altum, who worked for Chic in the winter doing snow removal and as a wrangler in the summer for the ranch. It wasn't too long before she came to work for Chic, who had offered her a job a few years earlier before she could leave her teaching job. Barb is another employee who has never left. She started in 1979 and is still working in the offices of Alta Ski Lifts. She loves Alta, the people, the mountains and the ski industry. Barb herself has never been a skier so her passion is more about the environment and the supportive relationships she has created over the years.

Even as busy as managing Alta Ski Lifts was on a daily basis, Chic and his managers found as they aged that they began to take longer and more relaxing lunches. Since Alta Ski Lifts housed many of their employees, they also had a dining room and fed them too. For most of the employees, that meant making a sandwich at breakfast and taking it with them on the mountain. But for those who were office-bound there were always sandwich makings and soup for lunch. Chic, Buck, Hans and Red would meet around the lunch hour. Somewhere along the line, they started playing cards—hearts. They often would play for more than an hour. The game and friendly banter between them were relaxing and amusing. Russ Harmer often said that the ski area could totally fall apart during those games and those four would still keep playing. When I was home visiting and skiing, I would stop by to say hello and listen to them. Often the only acknowledgment I got was a quick hello. After all, they were busy playing. Even after Chic retired, the four of them would get together and play at the house in Salt Lake City.

Chic was a tough man. After his hip accident when he was a boy, he was very rarely without some pain. When they replaced his hip, they took out almost two cups of bone chips. Over time, his femur had literally disintegrated and his limp became more and more pronounced. By the time he had his hip replaced, his bum leg was six inches shorter than his other one. This affected his back and knees, too. I believe, as do many of the people who worked with him over the years, that he was in chronic pain. Alan Engen told me that he often saw the pain on his face. Chic also suffered from acute migraine headaches. If medication didn't help, he had no other choice than to come home and wait it out. For Chic, his limp and the accompanying pain were just part of being active and it never stopped him from doing what he wanted or needed to do. Early on when he was working on the lifts he clambered up the lift towers as if nothing was a miss. Though he was very active when he wanted and needed to be, often after sitting for any amount of time, his hip would stiffen up and he would be slow getting up. His favorite expression was, "Oh, my aching backside, middle side and front side." Elfreda Shane recalls skiing High Rustler with Chic and his singing his way through his turns—a sure sign of a man who truly loved skiing and the adventure.

Chic was famous for his little "ditties." These were sayings that he repeated frequently. One of them was his food blessing: "Here's to the breezes that blow through the treezes and lifts the girls skirts above their kneezes. Thank God."

And there was, "We are off like wing tailed old birds."

"Oh dear, what can the matter be, seven old maids got locked in the lavatory. No one knew they were there."

"Balls," yelled the Queen, "if I had two I would be King."

I often find myself using these ditties as if he has never left us. In a way he never will.

CHAPTER #15

In closing

We miss my father, Chic Morton, as well, learned a great deal from him. We all craved his respect and dreaded the famous dark Chic look.

Chic lived a great deal of his life in physical discomfort and pain, which had a lot to do with his "grumpy" moods. He wasn't one to dwell on his discomfort, but I know that, over the years, it ate away at the pleasures he received from life. His chronic migraine headaches, which seemed to disappear after he retired, indicate to me that the stress of managing the Alta Ski Lifts also took its toll on him.

Of the many lessons he taught me, one was that, with great pleasures often comes great pain. Who would be wise enough to appreciate the pleasures without some pain? Another was that hurrying through things just brought you closer to the end, so slow down and enjoy all things.

The beautiful scenery of Alta has not changed, and the deep light powder still attracts thousands of skiers a year. Yet the mountains echo with the past of all the individuals that helped make it what it is today. Chic will be known for his strength of character, as well as keeping lift ticket prices low, the quality of the mountain skiing experience, his unwillingness to keep up with what other ski areas were doing, stating things as they were and giving hell when needed. His startling blue eyes, bald head and mischievous grin captivated all those who knew him. He was always quick to laugh, strike up a song, or whistle under his breath. His wise voice still whispers in many of our minds as we move through our lives.

Like many men in his generation, he wasn't one to show a great deal of emotion or share his thoughts. I noticed that in the last ten years of his life he became a softer and more gentle man. I surprised him on his 80th birthday with a watercolor painting done of me fly fishing in a local creek here in Colorado. He was thrilled and, besides his grin, he shed some tears. He had told both Jean and me several years before that he was going to die when he was 80. Surprised, I asked him how he had come up with that age. Well, he had averaged the age of his mother and his father when they had died and came up with 80. I warned him to be careful what he said that it might come true. Chic died seven months after his 80th birthday. He was a numbers man until the end.

Alta Ski Lifts threw Chic a big birthday bash for his 80th birthday at the Alta community center, the Lady of the Snow Chapel. Many of his old friends showed up and swapped old stories about skiing or Alta. It was festive, with people who loved him wandering through to give him hugs and wish him well. He grinned all afternoon. The cake they made for him was made to look like a chair lift chair with skis crossed on it. He got a chuckle out of that. On the daily lift tickets for November 24th, 1996 was printed, "CHIC MORTON SEXY SENIOR CITIZEN." His favorite girls, including Rosie at the ticket office, had made sure his name was honored that special day and he loved it.

After 51 years at Alta in July of 1997, Chic left us from cancer. I know he may still look over Alta, and he would be amazed at how much skiing has changed in the last 14 years, much less the last 50. One thing that hasn't changed though is the quality of the snow and the magic of Alta. Baldy Mountain still sits protectively over the glacier carved bowl, where Ballroom, Main Street, Mambo and Strawberry ski runs cradle skiers while they make their swooping turns down the mountain. Baldy's shoulder covets soft snow on steep slopes and the High Traverse gives access to tree-lined chutes for many vertical feet of powder turns. A few more trees have matured since those early days and the stands of fir and spruce are more robust but they still harbor secret stashes of Alta powder days after a storm.

The old lifts were slower and the powder snow stayed longer on the slopes. The Alta powder technique took skiers years to perfect with long straight skis; when it came, and a skier could link powder turns without falling, it was a gift from the gods of snow and an experience that every skier would try to reproduce for the rest of their lives. Powder snow is a gift, and Alta has an abundance of this light snow that could take skiers into another realm—one that worked

Chic at his 80th birthday party, hugs from Rosie and Tonia, November 1996.

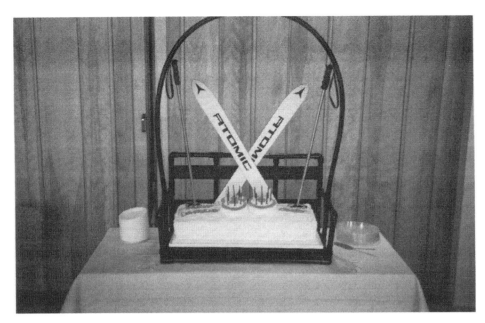

Chic's 80th birthday cake

with the forces of nature and required skier to be totally tuned into the snow, the mountain and their bodies. The most updated equipment has allowed many more skiers to become powder skiers more quickly, and the fresh untracked snow disappears with thousands of swooping ski tracks. The higher speed lifts take more people up the mountain, all vying for those powder stashes. It is a faster paced skiing than those early days. But the reality is that those powder turns still produce an ecstatic experience. Wooden skis, wooden towers and men of steel have morphed over time into fat skis, fast lifts and wild skiers.

Alta sees more skier visits daily and yearly than it did in the early days the road is open more often and, when the parking at Alta is full, skiers need to ride the bus or go elsewhere to ski. Many employees wind their way down the steep canyon to go home each night rather than live on the mountain. It is still Alta.

Some of the Alta folks who have been around since those early days believe there was more romance in the Alta Valley back then. If romance is the excitement, love and adventure of living and skiing in Alta, then there seems to be plenty of romance to be had in modern-day skiing at Alta. In those early days at Alta, there was a closeness that bred deep relationships mostly due to the isolation and the fact that everyone lived so closely together. Is it less romantic now or is it a different texture of romance? All I know for sure is that when I'm pointing my fancy powder skis down an untracked slope at Alta and I push off and feel that light snow move around my skis as I sink down and then it lifts me up again and snow flows around my body in a welcome embrace, I know there is no passage of time, only powder snow and Alta. It is still Alta. In his way, Chic will always have a piece of Alta that we will never forget.

AWARDS

Chic served as president of the Utah Ski Association, the Intermountain Ski Area Association and on the board of directors of the Forest Service Recreation Association.

1985 Chic was honored as the first member of the Tourism Hall of Fame.

1994 Chic received an award as a "Skisport Pioneer" from the United States Recreational Ski Association.

For his leadership, vision and many years of service to Utah skiing, Chic was the 1995 recipient of the S.J. and J.E. Quinney Award for outstanding achievement and contribution to Utah's Ski Industry.

Made in the USA
Charleston, SC
12 October 2012